P9-DGQ-187

Divided by a Common Language

A GUIDE TO BRITISH AND AMERICAN ENGLISH

⊰ Christopher Davies ⊱

Houghton Mifflin Company
Boston • New York

First Houghton Mifflin paperback edition 2007

Copyright © 2007, 2005, 1997 by Christopher Davies. All rights reserved.

An earlier version of this book was published by Mayflower Press, 1997.

No part of this work may be reproduced or transmitted in any form or by any means, electronic or mechanical, including photocopying and record- ing, or by any information storage or retrieval system without the prior written permission of Houghton Mifflin Company unless such copying is expressly permitted by federal copyright law. Address inquiries to Reference Permissions, Houghton Mifflin Company, 222 Berkeley Street, Boston, MA 02116.

Visit our website: www.houghtonmifflinbooks.com

Library of Congress Cataloging-in-Publication Data

Davies, Christopher, 1953–
    Divided by a common language : a guide to British and American
English / Christopher Davies.
        p. cm.
    An earlier version of this book was published as Divided by a common
language by Mayflower Press in 1997.
    Includes index.
    ISBN-13: 978-0-618-00275-7
    ISBN-10: 0-618-00275-8
    1. English language—Great Britain—Glossaries, vocabularies, etc.
    2. English language—United States—Glossaries, vocabularies, etc.
    3. English language—Variation—Great Britain—Handbooks, manuals,
etc. 4. English language—Variation—United States—Handbooks, manuals,
etc. 5. English language—Great Britain—Handbooks, manuals, etc.
    6. English language—United States—Handbooks, manuals, etc. I. Title.
    PE1704.D38 2005
    427—dc22
                                                                    2005005497

ISBN-13: 978-0-618-91162-2 (pbk.)
ISBN-10: 0-618-91162-6 (pbk.)

Manufactured in the United States of America

Book design by Catherine Hawkes, Cat & Mouse

MP 10 9 8 7 6 5 4 3 2 1

Table of Contents

Foreword

Since my first trip to the United States in 1979, I have been struck by the magnitude of the differences between British and American speech. Some experts estimate that there are roughly 4,000 words in everyday speech that are used differently. One might assume that Australia and New Zealand, for example, might have equally big differences in language and culture from their mother country, but not so. I found the differences in these two countries to be quite superficial in comparison with those of the United States. Of course slang expressions are quite different, but spelling and word usage are much the same. In fact recently, with Australian television shows being broadcast in Britain, some Australian slang is finding its way back home. By contrast, Canada, with its major cities all within a few hours' drive of the US border, has only a vestige of its British speech remaining in the English-speaking sections (though it still uses mostly British spelling), and to most outsiders Canada seems thoroughly American. The aim of this book is to give Americans and Britons a better understanding of each other's variation of the English language.

Acknowledgments

The author gratefully acknowledges the help and advice received from the Smithsonian Institution in Washington, DC, and from family and the many friends and acquaintances whose patience made this book possible.

Guide to Pronunciation and Other Symbols Used

Pronunciations given for words appear in square brackets throughout this book. The pronunciations offered here attempt to stay as close to the spelling as possible, but it is necessary to use some special symbols in some cases to specify the pronunciation clearly. The following special symbols and letter combinations are used throughout the book.

SYMBOLS	EXAMPLES
ă	*hat* [hăt]
ā *or* ay	*hate* [hāte], *trait* [trayt]
ah	*father* [**fah**·ther]
ə	*sofa* [**so**·fə]
ĕ	*bed* [bĕd]
ee *or* ē	*bead* [beed] or [bēd]
ĭ	*bit* [bĭt]
ī	*bite* [bīt]
ŏ	*cot* [kŏt] (in British pronunciations— most Americans say *pot* [paht])
ō *or* oh	*coat* [kōt], *adobe* [ə·**doh**·bee]
oo	*cool* [kool]
û	*cook* [kûk]
zh	*vision* [**vĭ**·zhən]

A raised dot [·] is used to separate syllables in a word, as for example in *tomato,* pronounced [to·**mā**·toh] or [to·**mah**·toh].

The accented (stressed) syllable in words of more than one syllable is put in boldface type.

Labels identify regionalisms and slang words (words used regularly only in a region within a country, such as the South in the US or Queensland in Australia). For example, an entry such as *rotary (regional New England)* means that in New England the word *rotary* is used instead of *traffic circle* (or *roundabout* in the UK).

In words lists comparing the vocabulary of two different varieties of English, words are listed in columns according to country. The addition plus sign (+) following a word indicates that the word or pronunciation is typical of the country represented by the column in which it appears, but it is also used and understood in the countries represented in the other column. When a plus sign (+) is found in both columns for a particular pair of words, it indicates that both terms are known in both countries, but that word given in the column is more common in the country described by that column. The asterisk (*) indicates that a word is discussed in Chapter 17, *Explanations,* on pages 220–227.

England and America are two countries divided by a common language.

attributed to
GEORGE BERNARD SHAW

⊰ 1 ⊱

How Did British and American English Become So Different?

A British reader looking at a newspaper or magazine from Australia or South Africa would not find too many unfamiliar words. Not so with American English. Words such as *clapboard, bleachers,* and *busboy* are everyday words in the US, but they would perplex the average speaker of British English. On the other hand, there are words used in British English that an American might find a little strange: *mailshot, crosspatch,* and *gymkhana.* (These words can all be found in the US–UK and UK–US lexicons in this book.)

Most English-speaking people are unaware of the vast differences between British and American English. This book is designed to enlighten the reader about these differences and briefly explain how these differences came about.

SOME ANSWERS

Why, when we have global communication on the Internet and we are all watching the same television shows, do we still have difficulty understanding one another? An estimated 4,000 words in everyday use in Britain have a different meaning or are used differently in the US. Let's go back in time to find some answers.

The early settlers in the US had no verbal contact with the folk they left behind in England, and the division of the language began. Over the years many Europeans settled in the US, bringing their languages with them. English remained the dominant language in America, although German was widely spoken in the 1800s. There were numerous French colonies, and New York was originally a Dutch settlement, called New Amsterdam. Each language left its mark on spoken English, with mainly the written word standardizing speech. Until the 1900s many books were imported from England, which did keep American English from straying too far.

Noah Webster, the well-known American lexicographer, forecast back in 1789 that eventually American English would be as different from British English as Dutch, Danish, and Swedish are from German, or from one another. This may sound preposterous, but Webster himself did initiate some of the biggest changes in American spelling. His *American Dictionary of the English Language* became the standard for spelling and word usage in America.

Webster, in his best-selling *American Speller*, published in 1783, suggested giving every letter in a syllable its due proportion of sound. Attitudes such as this may be responsible for some of the many pronunciation differences between American and British English. Other differences result from the fact that all languages change over time, and since the separation of the two varieties, American English has not changed in the same way as British English has changed. One example of a consistent pronunciation difference between British and American English can be heard in words ending with *–ary, –ory,* and *–ery*. In British English, the first vowel in the ending is not pronounced, as in the word *secretary*, usually four syllables in the US but often just three in the UK (that is, *secretary* is pronounced something like *secret'ry*).

British and American English probably reached their greatest divergence just before the Second World War and since that time have been getting closer, or at least better understood by the other country.

Here are some expressions currently used in the US that were once well known in Britain but have long since gone out of use there: *son of a gun, I guess, in back of* (for *behind*).

Another word no longer used in Britain but still used in the US is *gotten*, a past participle of the verb *to get*. In Britain, the usual past participle of *to get* is *got*. The only place where a Briton would use *gotten* is in the expression "Ill-gotten gains." But to the American ear, a sentence beginning "It has got to the point where . . ." sounds grammatically incorrect. Americans would say "It has gotten to the point where . . ." instead.

Still more words and phrases that have died out in Britain but are still used in the US are *turnpike* (for *toll road*), *fall* (for *autumn*), and *a deck of cards* (for *a pack of cards*). Conversely the words *straight away* meaning "immediately" and *presently* meaning "in a short time" are no longer in common usage in the US, but are often used in British English.

THE INDUSTRIAL REVOLUTION

Then along came the Industrial Revolution, bringing with it a need for many new words such as *railroad, windshield,* and *grade crossing*. The US was no longer conforming to the British standard with new words. Britain was already using other words: *railway, windscreen,* and *level crossing*.

Each country had its own engineers and designers, who gave new creations their particular names. Hundreds of new terms were needed. Of course these words were scarcely in print at the time, so there was no written standard to follow. With the countries so far apart there was really no need for the US to follow British usage. The differences increased as time went on, even though more people were traveling back and forth across the Atlantic by then. Many educated people were aware of the differences in terminology, but no great effort was made to unify the terms. The differences between British and American English gradually increased, until greater communication between the countries in the 1940s turned the tide. A good example of how far apart the languages had become is apparent in the list of railway terms (see page 70).

Despite all of the communication going on between Britain and the US today, it is amazing that new words being coined in one country are represented by another word in the other country. Some examples of relatively new American words and usages are *pound* (for the # symbol, as in "Press the pound key"), *beeper* (in the UK, a *bleeper*), and *cell phone* (in the UK, a *mobile phone*). Some newer British words that might not be understood by the average American are *video* (in the US, *VCR*), *flex* (in the US, *electrical cord*), and *bumf* (in the US, *unwanted papers and documents*).

The United States is a huge country. From the point of view of a Briton, it seems to have a surprisingly uniform speech pattern over a wide area if one considers its size. However, the United States has a diversity of accents and many different varieties of slang, much as Britain does. The lexicons in this book include many words that are particular to specific regions of the United States.

COUNTRIES THAT ENRICHED THE AMERICAN LANGUAGE

In order to understand why British English is so different from American English, it is necessary to learn something about the settlement of the United States. English was not the native tongue of many settlers in North America in the Colonial period. After the United States won its independence, immigrants from around the world continued to come to its shores. These immigrants have contributed many of the words that distinguish American English from British English.

France

Two hundred years ago, French rivaled English as the most widely used international language. There were several French colonies in North America. The largest, and the one that had the most influence on what would later become American English, was in the Mississippi Delta. The state of Louisiana gets its name from the French king Louis XIV. There are several different groups of French speakers in Louisiana. The French-speaking people known as the Cajuns came to Louisiana from Acadia, Nova Scotia. (Somewhere along the way *Acadians* became known as *Cajuns.*)

Here are some words the French settlers gave the English language: *bayou,* "a marshy inlet"; *gopher,* "a kind of burrowing rodent"; and *levee,* "dike." Here are a few French place names and their American pronunciations:

Versailles, in Kentucky	[ver·**sales**]
Des Moines, in Iowa	[duh·**moyn**]
St. Louis, in Missouri	[saint lewis]
Pierre, in South Dakota	[peer]
Terre Haute, in Indiana	[terra hote]

The Netherlands

By the mid-1600s, the Dutch had a large colony in what is now known as New York (originally New Amsterdam). The names of Brooklyn, Harlem, and the Bronx are all derived from Dutch. The Dutch left a legacy of the following words: *caboose, coleslaw, cookie,* and *waffle.*

Spain

The Spanish conquistadors left a hefty legacy of place names behind. In addition, they left Americans many words that are associated with cowboys these days, such as *lasso, mustang, rodeo,* and *burro.* Today the country's growing Latino population is creating what is called *Spanglish* in certain parts of the US.

Some words of Spanish origin that are everyday words in American English are

coyote, "a doglike wild animal"   [kie·**oh**·tee]
adobe, "a brick of clay and straw"   [a·**doh**·bee]
mesa, "a high piece of land"   [**may**·sa]

Here are a few Spanish place names and their American pronunciations:

La Jolla, in California   [la **hoy**·a]
El Cajon, in California   [el ca·**hone**]
La Quinta, in California   [la·**keen**·ta]
St. Augustine, in Florida   [saint **aug**·us·teen]

Germany

About seven million Germans have settled in the US. Not wishing to forget their country of origin, they have named twelve towns *Berlin* and seven *Germantown.* Germans have added a variety of words to American English, such as *bum* (shortened from *bummer,* from German *Bummler*) and the verb *to nix.*

Central European Countries

Many Jews from Central Europe settled in New York. Yiddish expressions are widely used in the US, but New York still leads the field in the use of these words. Here are some examples:

chutzpah	impudence/nerve
kibitz, to	give unsolicited advice/joke around
kosher	genuine/legitimate
klutz	clumsy person
schlep, to	trudge/lug
schmaltz	exaggerated sentimentalism
schmooze	chat/gossip
schnoz	a large nose
tush	backside

6

PRONOUNCING BRITISH PLACE NAMES

There are some cities and towns in England that are not pronounced phonetically. Here are a few examples:

Birmingham	[**bir**·ming·um]
Beaulieu	[**beeoo**·lee]
Bicester	[**bis**·ter]
Derby	[**dar**·bee]
Greenwich	[**gren**·ich]
Leicester	[**les**·ter]
Norwich	[**norr**·ich]
Warwick	[**worr**·ik]
Thames (the river)	[temz]

⊰ 2 ⊱

Tips For The Tourist

AT THE AIRPORT

Britons visiting the US or Americans visiting the UK will encounter different terms as soon as they step off the airplane (or *aeroplane* as the British say).

- A *jetway* in the US is a *boarding bridge* in the UK.
- A *skycap* in the US is an *airport porter* in the UK.
- A *baggage cart* in the US is called a *trolley* in the UK.
- One *hires* a car in the UK, and *rents* one in the US.
- It's a taxi *rank* in the UK, rather than a taxi *stand.*

Did you know that English is the international language of aviation, but terms used in the US are different? If a pilot is requested to circle the airport in the US, he is asked to do a *360-degree.* In the rest of the world a pilot is requested to make an *orbit.*

AT THE HOTEL

In the US, the floor of a building level with the ground is known as the *first floor;* in Britain it is called the *ground floor.* What is known in the US as the *second floor* is called the *first floor* in Britain; the *third floor* in the US is called the *second floor* in Britain; and so forth. An *efficiency* in the US is a room with a small kitchen as well as a bathroom. The widely-used British hotel term *en-suite,* meaning "with a private bathroom," is not understood in the US. *Duvets,* which are found everywhere in Britain, are not at all common in the US. In a British hotel or bed-and-breakfast establishment, you may be offered *half board.* This is similar to the US term *American plan,* i.e., breakfast and dinner are included in the price. Motels are not common in England. Traveler's hotels are similar and they often use the word *lodge* in their name. Many more moderately priced British hotels will have rooms with a shared bathroom, and often no television or telephone in the room. They have a lounge with a television, and often a dining room. Curiously the word *accommodation* is never used in the plural in British English. In the US you make arrangements for *accommodations.*

Some British hotel terms can cause confusion for Americans:

- *Reception* means *front desk.*
- A *receptionist* is a *desk clerk.*
- A *flannel* is a *washcloth.*
- A *cot* means a *crib.*
- A *communicating door* is a *connecting door.*
- *Tariff* means *rate.*

Additionally, in Britain a faucet is called a *tap,* a twin bed is called a *single bed,* and a rollaway bed is known as a *fold-up bed.* In the US another term for a double bed is a *full-size bed.*

⊰ 3 ⊱

Practical Information

AUTOMOBILES

The British Automobile

British rental cars do not usually come with automatic transmission unless you specifically request it. They are small by American standards but many do have air conditioning. All British cars have signal lights called *repeaters* on the side of the car. They come on when you signal that you are turning and allow the drivers of cars alongside you to be aware of your intentions. Controls on British cars are generally similar to American cars these days, but of course one drives a car sitting on the right. British cars come with a hand brake for parking, never a foot-operated parking brake. Diesel cars are now popular in the UK. Diesel hoses at the pump are black—petrol hoses are green.

The American Automobile

All rental cars in the US have automatic transmission and air conditioning as standard equipment, and all but the smallest, known as *subcompacts,* will have power steering and power brakes. Manual transmission is usually available upon request. Compact cars are probably as big as the average British car. Mid-size and full-size cars will seem quite roomy, but the huge cars that were common in the 1970s are a thing of the past. The suv (sport-utility vehicle) has taken over the task of moving large families from one place to another.

Here are some words of advice for British drivers in the us. It is the law in most states to wear a seat belt when sitting in the front seat of an automobile. In some cars you may not be able to shift out of park without first putting your foot on the brake pedal. You will not find a hand brake in larger cars. These will be equipped with a parking brake pedal, located at the upper far left of the driver's left leg. Once engaged, the parking brake will remain set until it is released manually, usually by pulling the lever marked "brake release" located under the dashboard just above the parking brake pedal. In some cars, the parking brake is automatically released when you shift out of park. The parking brake pedal is equivalent to a hand brake, which is found in some smaller cars. Americans often refer to this brake as the *emergency brake*. The automatic transmission selector or *gearshift* is situated either on the steering column or on a console between the driver and passenger seats. Often, the key cannot be removed unless the selector is in park. In the us one *rolls down* a car window; in the UK one *winds down* the window.

GASOLINE (PETROL)

There are two grades of petrol (gasoline) commonly available in Britain today; premium unleaded is about 95 octane and super unleaded is about 98 octane. Premium unleaded, despite its name, has the lower octane, but it is suitable for most modern cars. Petrol is sold by the litre (liter).

All gas in the us is unleaded. It comes in three grades: regular, which is 87 octane; a middle grade of 89 octane, also known as unleaded plus; and premium or super, which may be as high as 94 octane, depending on the brand. Gasoline is still sold by the gallon in the us and is incredibly cheap by European standards. The us gallon is based on a 16-ounce pint, rather than the British

20-ounce pint, and therefore is smaller. A US gallon is just under four liters. Americans sometimes use the colloquial expression *to gas up* a vehicle, meaning to refuel it. Payment can usually be made with a credit card at the pump.

TELEPHONES

British Telephones

Public telephones in Britain are mainly operated by British Telecom (BT). Local calls are not unlimited for a flat rate as they often are in the US. Some British pay phones will accept a variety of coins, but many require a *phone card* or *charge card.* Phone cards are readily available at shops and post offices in varying denominations. They are inserted into a slot on the phone and a display tells you how much value remains on the card. The card is thrown away when its value is zero. If you have a telephone account with British Telecom, you can obtain a BT charge card, which enables you to bill a call to your account from any telephone. Long-distance calls in Britain always start with the number 0. Local calls from a private home or business are usually charged by the minute. This naturally cuts down on telephone solicitation. However, evening and week-end rates are low and even free if you sign up with certain companies. A toll-free long-distance number is known as a *Freefone* or *Freephone* number, and usually starts with 0-800, 0-808, or 0-500. The British phones ring with a distinctive double ring. An area code, formerly known as an *STD code* (*subscriber trunk dialling code*), is often called a *phone code* or a *dial code.*

American Telephones

A local call from a US pay phone is on average 35 cents for the first three minutes. Usually you pick up the handset, put in the money, and then dial the number. Some independently owned pay phones require you to dial the number first, then deposit the money. There is often no time limit on local calls. The ringing tone is distinctive, because American phones do not ring with a double ring as do the British phones.

Local calls from a private phone are often free. Long-distance calls always start with the digit 1. Just because a number happens to be in the same area code as the one you are calling from doesn't mean that it is a local call. You may well have to dial 1 followed by the same area code and then the number you want, in order to reach that number. A recording will tell you if it is necessary to do this. To make a long-distance call from a pay phone using coins, dial 1, then the area code followed by the number. You will then hear a recording instructing you on how much money to deposit for a three-minute conversation.

There are no nationally available phone cards like those in the United Kingdom, but in some locations and at all airports, you will find phones that do accept *calling cards*. There are two major types of calling cards: those provided by a long distance carrier, with charges billed to your account, and prepaid phone cards that can be purchased at various shops. Most calling cards require you first to dial the company's toll-free number found on the card, then your account number, prior to dialing the number you want. With prepaid cards, charges are deducted until the card expires. Calling cards make long-distance phoning from a pay phone much easier.

Many businesses have *toll-free* numbers, which require dialing 1-800, 1-877, or 1-888 before the exchange number. These toll-free numbers, popularly known as *800 numbers,* are more common in the US than in Britain. Beware of the letter *o*. It is not the same key as the number o in the US. The abbreviation *Ph.* is often used for "telephone number" in the US as well as *Tel.*

Here are some comparisons of terms from the US and the UK relating to telephones.

- The symbol #, known as *pound* in the US, is called *hash* or *square* in the UK.

13

- *Caller ID* in the US is known as *caller display* in the UK.
- *Call forwarding* in the US is known as *call diversion* in the UK.
- A *calling card* is similar to the BT *charge card.*
- A *busy signal* in the US is known as an *engaged signal* in the UK.
- A *dial tone* is known in British English as a *dialling tone.*
- An *unlisted number* is known in British English as an *ex-directory number.*
- *Directory assistance* or *information* are known as *directory inquiries* in the UK.

⊰ 4 ⊱

For The Technically Minded

PLUMBING

The plumbing system and plumbing terminology in Britain differ slightly from their US counterparts. A *trap,* or *P-trap* to be more precise, sits below the sink in the US. This device is known as a *U-bend* in Britain, where the word *tap* is used for both indoor and outdoor plumbing. In the US, indoor taps are known as *faucets,* and outdoor taps are known as *spigots.* The term *tap water* is used in both countries, however. In the US, the cold faucet is uniformly on the right for safety reasons. This is not true in Britain, where it can be found on either side. Household hot-water systems differ slightly. In Britain, the hot-water tank (known as a *cistern*), is usually fed from a tank in the attic, so that an overheated tank cannot blow back into the main supply line. In the US, hot-water tanks are fed directly from the water supply (known as the *mains* in Britain) to the house. Thus the hot and cold water are at the same pressure, making mixer taps almost standard and very convenient.

Toilets in the US, though similar in appearance, have major differences. The equipment in the tank (known as a *cistern* in Britain) is very simple, consisting of a float and stop valve for maintaining the water level in the tank, and a rubber seal, known as a *flapper,* which sits over the outlet pipe at the bottom of the tank. The flapper is connected by a chain to the handle. When the handle is pushed down, it pulls up the chain, in turn raising the flapper and releasing the water. The system works admirably, but as the flapper ages it does not always maintain a good seal, resulting in a waste of water. For this reason, this system is not permitted in Britain, where a diaphragm is used to start a siphon effect from the tank into the bowl. In the US, the toilet bowls are all of the siphonic type. As the tank empties into the bowl, a siphon effect forms in the S bend in the base of the toilet, resulting in a rapid emptying of the bowl, followed by a gurgle. This system gives a good flush and is reasonably quiet but tends to block up more readily than the standard British system that relies solely on a rush of water.

ELECTRICITY

In the US, electricity at the electrical outlet is 120 volts AC, 60 hertz. Plugs are mostly two-pin, or three-pin if they have a *ground pin.* Outlets are usually paired, one above the other. There are two vertical slots with a hole below for the ground. Older two-slot outlets with no ground are still found in older buildings. Appliances are fitted with a molded plug. With high-wattage appliances, it is normal for the plug to get warm! Most kitchen appliances have only two flat pins. To make them safer, one pin is slightly wider than the other, and the outlet also has different slot sizes so that the plug can only be inserted right way up. These plugs are called *polarized* plugs. This way the appliance gets current only as far as its switch, until it is turned on. Refrigerators and microwave ovens, however, are all fitted with a ground pin. Light bulbs have a screw fitting rather than the British bayonet fitting, although the bayonet type is used in cars. Some light bulbs have two filaments, giving a possibility of three levels of brightness. These are known as *three-way bulbs.*

Electricity is usually carried to houses on overhead wires. Although this system cuts distribution costs, it does result in more weather-related power failures, often called power *outages*. High-tension lines are supported by *towers*, or quite commonly, tall poles. All houses are equipped with two 120-volt lines in opposing phases. This enables 240 volts to be used for appliances, such as water heaters, kitchen stoves, and dryers. These plugs and outlets are not the same as the 120-volt plugs and outlets. Light-switch positions are down for off, up for on.

In Britain, electricity comes to the house through underground wires at 240 volts on one phase. Light switches go down for on, up for off. Electrical outlets are usually paired side by side. The *earth pin* (*ground pin* in the US) on plugs is larger and longer than the other pins, and as it enters the matching hole in the socket, it raises the cover over the other two pins, permitting them to go in. All appliances are either *earthed* (*grounded*), or double insulated for safety. Light bulbs often have a bayonet fitting, rather than a screw fitting as is normal in the US. The support towers that carry power across the country at high voltages are known as *pylons*. The supply of electricity to the house is referred to as the *mains*, just like the water supply mentioned earlier. Hence a small appliance may be either battery or *mains* operated.

The word *mains* is not used or understood in the US for electricity in the house, or for water or gas supplies (see Explanations, page 224).

Instant water heaters are in common use for showers in the UK. They are known as *power showers*.

A *G.F.I.* protector (Ground Fault Interrupter) in an electrical circuit is known as an *R.C.B.* breaker (Residual Circuit Breaker). High speed internet access via a phone line is known as *DSL* in the US and *ADSL* in the UK.

❧ 5 ❧

Institutions and Services

Rather than presenting a table of British English/American English comparisons, I have chosen to give a brief description of various institutions. Terms that may be unfamiliar to Americans or Britons are given in italics.

THE POSTAL SYSTEM

The British Postal Service

The postal service in Britain is known as the *Royal Mail,* and the monarch's head appears on every stamp. The letter carrier, or postman, delivers mail once a day on foot in the cities and suburbs. Until recently, there were two deliveries a day. Letter carriers wear black boots, a navy blue uniform, and a badge with a crown that says *Royal Mail.* Temporary letter carriers do not wear a uniform, but wear an armband with the words *Royal Mail* on it.

Letters can go first-class or second-class. The stamps for first-class mail are more expensive but should guarantee next-day delivery. Second-class mail may take a few days. House numbers progress in numerical order, with even-numbered houses on one side of the street and odd-numbered houses on the other. Mail within Britain is called *inland mail.*

The *postcode* was devised around 1970 and consists of a combination of letters and numbers such as AB2 2BA. It is similar to the American *Zip Code* and goes on the last line of the address.

Mail that has the postage imprinted on it by machine is known as *franked mail.* In the US this is called *metered mail.* If a record of the receipt of the letter is required, one asks for *recorded delivery.* A *money order* is known as a *postal order* in the UK.

Books of stamps may be purchased at petrol stations or newsagents, as well as post offices.

The US Postal Service

The American letter carrier, also known as the mailman or mail carrier, wears a blue uniform, which in the summer may consist of a short-sleeve shirt, short trousers, and knee socks. Mail delivery is much the same as in Britain, especially in cities and larger towns. However, in many suburbs and in all rural areas mail carriers drive a white jeep with the steering wheel on the "wrong" side. This enables them to deliver and retrieve mail easily at each house by pulling alongside *mailboxes* set on posts standing at the side of each driveway. Attached to the mailbox is a red piece of metal, commonly called a flag, which is set in a vertical position to indicate that there are letters in the box for the mail carrier to retrieve and post. There are not many public mailboxes available in rural areas. Where available, they are large, blue, freestanding metal boxes that have a combination receptacle/door at the top that pulls open. After letters are deposited on the door, it is closed, and the door drops the letter into the box. *Express mail* is faster than *priority mail.* American mail carriers have a *route* (a fixed course or area in which they deliver mail). There is only one delivery a day, six days a week.

To facilitate mail delivery, the Zip Code, an acronym for *Zoning Improvement Plan,* was introduced in 1963 and is required on each piece of mail. It consists of five numbers, a hyphen, and then four numbers. The last four numbers are often omitted, even though they do facilitate the handling of mail within their designated zone. It will soon be compulsory to use all nine numbers. Two letters, indicating the state, precede the Zip Code.

Stamps may be purchased not only at the post office but also at vending machines, although the price is slightly higher. Post office vending machines sell stamps at face value. Most supermarkets also sell stamps. Small post offices abound, just as in Britain, and you rarely have to wait long to be served. Except in large cities, you won't find any glass partition between you and the clerk. This is true for banks as well. If you wish to have a receipt from the party you are mailing to, you must ask to send the mail *return receipt requested.* Mail sent and delivered entirely within the US is known as *domestic mail.*

BANKING

British and American banks do not differ much these days. One big difference is that Americans do a lot of their banking at *drive-throughs.* Most banks have several drive-through lanes in which a pneumatic cylinder whisks your checks (spelled *cheques* in Britain), papers, and money into the bank (although too many coins in the cylinder can produce a rather interesting effect as they climb up the clear plastic tube). A short while later the cylinder returns with either money or a deposit slip and a voice through the speaker wishes you a nice day. Remember to put the cylinder back before driving off! A United States driving license, which has one's photo on it, is often required for proof of identity (ID) in the US. A British or American tourist will need a passport for proof of identity. Most British credit cards can be used at a cash machine (ATM) to withdraw dollars, but you will need your PIN number.

Below is a comparison of some American banking terms with some used in Britain.

- A *savings and loan* (commonly abbreviated S&L) is similar to a British *building society.*

- A *mutual fund* is known in Britain as a *unit trust*.
- *Common stocks* are known as *ordinary shares*.
- A *checking account* is also called a *current account*.
- A *savings account* is known as a *deposit account*.
- A *deposit slip* is known as a *credit slip*.
- A *routing number* is known as a *branch sort code*.
- A *checkbook register* is known as a *transaction record book* (although it is usually part of the checkbook in the UK).
- A *money market account* is known as a *high interest account*.
- CDs (*certificates of deposit*) are known as *savings certificates* in Britain.
- An ATM is called a *cash machine* in the UK.
- A *stub* on a check is also known as a *counterfoil* in Britain.

THE CURRENCY

British Money

In Britain all the currency *notes* (pieces of paper currency) are of a different size, and the higher the denomination, the larger the note. Different denominations also have different colors, so they cannot easily be confused. A five-pound note is known colloquially as a *fiver*, and a ten-pound note as a *tenner*. The monarch's head is on every note, the denominations being 5, 10, 20, and 50. The notes are changed every few years and a different design is used to prevent counterfeiting. Such units of currency as guineas, shillings, half crowns, florins, and farthings no longer exist. In the traditional system in use since the eleventh century, one pound equaled 20 shillings, and one shilling equaled 12 pennies. There were thus 240 pence in a pound. On February 15, 1971, a decimal system for the division of the pound was adopted, with 100 pennies to the pound. These pennies were called *new pence*.

The current silver coins have recently changed and have no pet names at this time. A *bob* was the slang term for a shilling. A *tanner* used to be the equivalent of six pence or half a shilling. The *halfpenny*, pronounced [**hay**·pnee] is no longer legal tender, nor is the *farthing*, a quarter of a penny, which was withdrawn in 1961. A *guinea* was worth one pound and a shilling, and was used when paying fees to professionals. The plural of *penny* is *pence*: *one penny*, but *two pence*, formerly pronounced [**tupp**·əns]. The symbol £ stands for pounds, p for pence. The one-pound note has been replaced by the pound coin. (Scotland uses the Scottish pound, which is equivalent in value to the British pound, and accepted all over the UK. However, the notes and coins differ in appearance from the British notes. Unlike the British pound, the Scottish pound is still issued in a one-pound note in addition to a one-pound coin.)

If an article costs £1.65, it would be spoken "one pound sixty five." The pound is also referred to as the *pound sterling*. A slang term for a pound is a *quid*. Pounds (lbs.) are also a unit of weight in Britain, though the metric system is becoming widely used now.

American Money

In the US, currency notes are called *bills* and are all the same size and color (green), hence the slang term *greenback*. They differ mainly in the pictures on the bill (mostly former US presidents) and the denomination, which is written in all four corners. It is advisable, therefore, to check the denomination of each bill carefully before spending it. American men often carry their bills in a *billfold*, a type of wallet, or in a *money clip*. The most circulated denominations are one, five, ten, twenty, fifty and one hundred. Very rarely you may come across a two-dollar bill. These were originally known as deuces and were reintroduced into circulation in the 1970s, along with a dollar coin called the Susan B. Anthony dollar. Although both the two-dollar bill and the Susan B. Anthony dollar coin are legal tender, neither one is in popular use. In 2000 a gold-colored dollar coin, the Sacagawea dollar, was introduced with no better results. Americans tend to be resistant to any change in matters of money, miles, or gallons. The four most common coins in use have been around for a long time. The one-cent coin is called a *penny* and is similar in color and size to the British penny. The five-cent coin is called a *nickel.* It is silver in color and is roughly the size of a 20p coin. The *dime,* worth ten cents, is a tiny silver coin. The twenty-five cent coin is commonly called a *quarter,* and is the same size and color as the new 10p coin. As in Britain, coins are often referred to as *change.* If an article costs $1.65, the price would be read "a dollar sixty five." The symbol o (zero) is often read as "oh," and $2.05 would be pronounced "two oh five." The $ symbol comes before the dollar amount, and the ¢ symbol is placed after the cents if the amount is under a dollar (e.g., 79¢).

Buck is a very common informal word for "dollar," heard in such sentences as *Can you lend me a few bucks?* or *It cost about a buck fifty* ($1.50). The bills used to have names, often inspired by the Roman numerals on the corners, but these are no longer in common use. The two was known as a *deuce,* the five as a *fin,* the ten as a *sawbuck* (inspired by the Roman numeral X on each corner, which looks like a sawhorse, also known as a sawbuck in the US). The hundred-dollar bill was known as a *C-note* (from the Roman numeral C on each corner of the earlier bills).

RESTAURANTS

The American Restaurant

Restaurants are plentiful and quite reasonable in the US. Americans tend to eat out more than the British. Very often Americans will give directions using restaurants as landmarks. There are many restaurant chains, which serve the same fare wherever you go. To some, this uniformity may seem boring; to others it may provide a sense of security. Service tends to be good, as food servers rely on tips to make a decent income. Tipping is expected. Fifteen to twenty percent is considered a basic tip throughout most of the United States. The tip is left at the table. An easy way to calculate an 18% tip is to divide the bill by six.

There are quite a few restaurants that serve buffet-style meals. Even at these, if you are waited on in any way, a tip is appropriate—perhaps 10%. Salad bars are common and usually quite extensive. Salad dressings come in many flavors. Often fruit and soup will be served at a salad bar, and even assorted flavored jellies, which in Britain might be considered a dessert.

Sandwiches, which are enormous and are often a meal in themselves, are on the menu in many restaurants. They are usually served with a pickle and some chips or crisps (*fries* or *chips* in the US). You may state what kind of bread you would like (white, whole wheat, pumpernickel, or rye) and whether or not you would like it toasted. Sandwiches often consist of meat, lettuce and tomato, and mayonnaise. A *melt,* such as a *tuna melt,* is topped with cheese that is melted under a broiler or in a toaster oven. If you see the phrase *à la mode* on the dessert menu, it means "with ice cream." Some of the more interesting food names are *Buffalo wings, sloppy Joes,* and *pigs in a blanket* (for definitions see pages 26, 27, and 28). The servers often say "Enjoy!" after bringing your meal. It's short for "Enjoy your meal!" The main course is known as the *entrée,* the starter as the *appetizer,* and the sweet or pudding is only known as *dessert.* (*Pudding* in the US means a kind of soft custard.) The UK term *jacket potatoes* may not be understood. Ask for *baked potatoes.* In a fast-food restaurant you will hear the term *hold* used when a dish is ordered without a certain item, e.g., "Hold the onions."

Hot tea is available, but in the South you must specify that you want hot tea, since iced tea is more common. Hot tea usually comes as a pot of hot water, a tea bag, and a sturdy-looking cup. Quite often you will get tiny prepackaged containers of cream (*half-and-half*) instead of milk, so remember to specify milk or lemon, as desired. Soft drinks are served with lots of ice, especially in the summer. *Root beer* is a dark soft drink made with juices extracted from roots, herbs, and bark. A *smoothie* is a drink of milk with blended fruits (usually bananas are the base).

Americans eat their food with the fork held in the right hand and the tines up, while Britons and other Europeans hold it in the left hand, tines down. The origin of these differences in the use of eating utensils is disputed. Soupspoons in the US tend to be smaller than those used in Britain, and desserts are eaten with a small spoon or a fork. (A *dessert spoon* is not used as a unit of measure in the US.) *Broiled* means grilled. You will sometimes encounter the term *broasted*. Broasted food has been cooked in a high-pressure fryer made by the Broaster Company.

Here are some British/American equivalents:

- Cutlery is usually called *flatware* or *silverware* in the US.
- A *serviette* is called a *napkin*.
- *Takeaway* food is known as *takeout* food in the US.
- A *salt cellar* is called a *salt shaker*.
- The *head waiter* is known as the *maitre d'*.
- The *wine waiter* is known as the *wine steward*.
- If you wish to take any food home with you, ask for a *box*, or a *doggy bag* (although this term is dying out).
- When you are ready for the bill, ask for the *check*.

The many ethnic groups that settled in the US have naturally influenced American food. Here are some explanations of some strange-sounding foods you may see on American menus:

Some American Foods

apple brown Betty (or *apple Betty*)	apple crumble
bagel	a bread roll in a doughnut shape
blackened food	food cooked over a strong flame, very spicy

For a guide to pronunciation symbols, see page vi.

bologna [bə·**loh**·nee]	smoked, seasoned sausage
Buffalo wings	spicy chicken wings (first named in the Anchor Bar, Buffalo, NY)
burrito [bu·**ree**·toh]	meat and refried beans rolled in a tortilla (Mexican)
caesar salad	a salad consisting of romaine lettuce, grated cheese, croutons, anchovies, raw egg, and olive oil
chowder	a thick soup of clams, fish, or vegetables usually containing potatoes and milk
club sandwich	a double-decker sandwich filled with meat (usually chicken or turkey), together with tomato, lettuce, and mayonnaise
cobbler	fruit with pastry on top, cooked in a low pan
coffeecake	a flat glazed cake or sweetened bread (no coffee in it)
corn bread	bread made from cornmeal, usually baked in small loaves
corned beef	beef cured in brine, then cooked
crêpe	pancake
Dagwood	a thick sandwich filled with different types of meat, some cheese, and condiments
English muffin	something like a crumpet in appearance, but made from a light dough, usually served toasted at breakfast
flapjack	a thick pancake, quite unlike British flapjack (oats mixed with syrup)
fried eggs	these are ordered "over easy," "over hard," or "sunny side up"
grits	cornmeal cooked with water, usually served as a side dish at breakfast (Southern)

gumbo	a soup thickened with okra pods, usually found in the South
gyro	sliced beef or lamb served as a sandwich on pita bread (also called a *gyros*)
hash browns	shredded or diced potatoes, which are then fried
hoagie/sub/ submarine	meat and salad in a long bread roll (also known as a hero)
home fries	boiled potatoes that have been sliced and then fried
hush puppies	balls of fried corn meal (so called because they were originally fed to the dogs to keep them quiet)
links	breakfast sausages (sausages are also served as patties)
lox	salmon cured in brine
nachos [**nah**·chōz]	fried corn tortilla chips covered with some combination of melted cheese, salsa, or beans
pancakes/ hot cakes	thick pancakes served for breakfast with butter and syrup
pastrami	seasoned smoked beef
pigs in a blanket	frankfurters baked in pastry/sausages rolled in pancakes
pretzel	hard dough twisted into a fancy shape and salted, usually served as a snack
Reuben	a grilled sandwich of corned beef, Swiss cheese, and sauerkraut, usually made with rye bread (named after Arnold Reuben, Jr., who owned Reuben's Restaurant in New York)
Salisbury steak	minced steak made into a rectangular patty and covered with gravy
scrod	immature cod or haddock (weighing between 1½ and 2½ lbs)

sloppy Joe	barbecued beef, often on an open bun
succotash	beans (usually lima beans) and corn served together
sweet roll	a roll made with sweetened dough containing raisins and candied fruit, often topped with icing
taco [**tah**·coh]	a Mexican food consisting of minced meat, tomatoes, cheese, and onion in a hard crusty tortilla
tamale [tə·**mah**·lee]	well-seasoned minced meat, packed in cornmeal dough then wrapped in cornhusks and steamed
tortilla [tor·**tee**·ya]	thin flour or corn pancakes, a Mexican staple
waffles	light cakes made from batter cooked in a waffle iron to give it a honeycomb appearance, served for breakfast with hot syrup
Waldorf salad	chopped apple, nuts, and celery mixed with mayonnaise

The British Restaurant

British restaurants are more individual than their US counterparts. Tipping is less standardized, and often in a casual restaurant there is a jar for tips at the counter. Fifteen percent would be a generous tip. There are many teahouses in small towns and villages. There one can have *high tea* in the afternoon. This consists of sandwiches, scones and perhaps a light, cooked meal, usually served with a cup of tea. Sandwiches are usually small with a thin filling. Sherry trifle is sometimes served with high tea. It consists of fruit, sherry-soaked sponge cake, and sometimes jelly, topped with a custard sauce.

In a restaurant the entrée is often called the *main course,* and the appetizer the *starter.* Dessert may be called *sweet* or *pudding.* If you have lunch in a pub you will probably be offered a *ploughman's lunch,* consisting of a hunk of bread, ham, cheese, and some pickles.

Here are explanations of some strange-sounding foods you may encounter in Britain.

Some British Foods

bangers and mash	a slang term for sausages and mashed potato
black pudding	a black link sausage containing pork, suet, and pigs' blood
bubble and squeak	mashed potato and vegetables formed into a patty and fried
corned beef	processed canned beef
crumpet	made from a yeast mixture, similar in appearance to an English muffin, but doughy
Eccles cake	a flat cake made of pastry filled with currants
fool	a cold dessert of crushed fruit blended with cream or custard
gateau [**gă**·toh]	any type of rich cake
kippers	smoked herring
lemon curd/ lemon cheese	a preserve made from lemon, eggs, sugar, and butter
Marmite	a dark, salty vegetable and yeast extract spread on bread
pease [peez] *pudding*	split peas boiled with carrots and onions
pikelet [**pĭk**·let]	similar to a thin crumpet
ploughman's lunch	bread, cheese, and a pickle or salad, often served in a pub
pork pie	minced pork covered in pastry (usually about the size of a cupcake), eaten cold

For a guide to pronunciation symbols and other signs, see page vi.

rissole	ground meat and spices, covered in bread crumbs and fried
sago pudding	a dessert similar to tapioca pudding, made from starch from the sago palm
Scotch egg	a hard-boiled egg covered in sausage meat and deep fried
spotted dick	a sponge or suet pudding with currants in it
steak and kidney pudding	chopped steak and kidney steamed in a pudding basin (bowl) lined with pastry
summer pudding	bread and fresh fruit allowed to set in a pudding bowl
toad in the hole	link sausages baked in a pan of batter
Yorkshire pudding	batter baked in a flat pan, usually served with roast beef

BARS

Beer is not ordered by quantity in the US. One asks for beer, either on tap, in a can, or in a bottle. If you do not specify how much you want, the bartender (usually *barman* in the UK) will choose for you. In Britain one orders a pint or half-pint. A variety of beer brands are available in most bars in both countries. There are three principal types of beer sold in Britain: *bitter, lager,* and *stout.* Bitter is a darkish-colored beer, usually served at room or cellar temperature; it has a fruity taste. Some pubs still serve this from barrels—beer served in this way from small breweries is known as *real ale.* Lager, a pale-colored beer favored by the younger generation, is often served chilled and may have a continental European name signifying its origin. Most American beers would be classified in this category. Stout is a strong, dark beer. The most famous stout is Guinness. Most cocktails are pretty international, but you may like to try a local mix. If no mixer is to be added, drinks are ordered *straight up* in the US and *neat* in Britain. A *shandy* in Britain is half beer and half lemonade. A *liqueur* is also known as a *cordial* in the US. It is customary to leave the bartender a small tip in the US, but not in Britain. Toasts are similar in both countries. Cider is always alcoholic in the UK. In the US, on the other hand, cider (also known as apple cider or sweet cider) is not alcoholic, but *hard cider* is fermented and contains alcohol.

Here are some common American drinks defined:

- A *daiquiri* contains rum and lemon mix.
- A *highball* contains spirits and water or a soft drink and is served in a tall glass.
- A *Manhattan* contains whiskey, sweet vermouth, and bitters.
- A *piña colada* is made of pineapple juice, rum, and coconut.
- A *Tom Collins* contains gin, lemon mix, and soda water.
- *Long Island iced tea* is not as innocent as the name might suggest. It is a strong alcoholic drink the color of iced tea containing rum, tequila, gin, and vodka.
- A *mimosa* (champagne and orange juice) is called *Buck's Fizz* in Britain.

SHOPPING

In Britain

Many small British shops are independently owned, and there may be accommodations above the shop. VAT (value added tax), similar to sales tax in the US but higher, is included in the purchase price. No VAT is levied on uncooked food, books, or newspapers. Large American-style supermarkets are now very common. Sometimes they are built out in the country in order to provide sufficient parking space for the customers. It is not usual to have your groceries bagged, although larger supermarkets will now bag groceries on request. Plastic bags are provided for your use however. A canvas awning often extends out from small shops to protect the customers from inclement weather. Shopping hours tend to be shorter than in the US. In Britain, the register is usually called the *till,* and *early closing* means a day when shops close in the afternoon. A shopping cart is known as a *shopping trolley,* and bags of groceries are always referred to as *shopping.*

In the US

In the US your groceries are bagged for you at the checkout, and you may be offered assistance in carrying your groceries to the car. A sales tax, similar to VAT, is added at the register to all items, with the exception of unprepared food and medications in some states. This means the price marked on the product is not the price you pay at the register. The amount of this tax, a percentage of the price, varies from state to state and even from county to county within the state. When speaking about making a purchase, Americans are quite specific about where they are going. If they are going to the supermarket, Americans will say they are going to the *market* (supermarket), or going *grocery shopping* at the *grocery* or *grocery store.* Brits just go *shopping* at the shops for groceries or anything else.

Fresh foods are found in the *produce* [**prō**·doos] department, milk is found in the *dairy case,* and butter is sold in *sticks,* with four 4-ounce sticks in a box. *Soda water* is usually known as *club soda* (which may contain some trace potassium compounds) or *seltzer water* (pure carbonated water). A surprising number of English foods may be purchased in American supermarkets.

Shopping malls are the popular way to shop in the States. With huge parking areas, these may cover several acres and be on several levels. Many items of clothing and shoes are known by different names. Note that shoe sizes are slightly different. For British shoppers to find the corresponding size in American shoe stores, they should add a size and a half to women's shoes and a half size to men's shoes. Men's shirts go by the same sizes, although long sleeve shirts have various sleeve lengths. Women's dress sizes are different. A UK size 10 is a US size 8 for example. Now that metric sizes have arrived in Britain, comparisons will be different.

Factory outlet malls, usually located by highways, are popular with the US shopper. They consist of stores selling selected brand names in clothing and household items at reduced prices. In American malls, a shop assistant is known as a *salesperson*, haberdashery is called *notions*, and outsize clothing is *extra large* or *XL*.

PRONUNCIATION OF FOOD NAMES

The names of some foods are pronounced differently in the US and the UK, as you may discover if you ask the person serving you to describe an item on the menu in a restaurant. The American pronunciation of the word *herb* is actually the original one. *Herb* is one of a group of English words of French origin, like *honor* or *hour*, in which the *h* is silent. The *h* was reintroduced in pronunciation in the UK during the nineteenth century under the influence of the spelling of the word.

Differences in the Pronunciation of Food Names

WORD	US PRONUNCIATION	UK PRONUNCIATION
apricot	ă·pri·cot	ā·pri·cot
basil	bā·zil	bă·zil
fillet	fil·lay	fill·et
herb	erb	herb
oregano	or·eh·ga·no	or·a·gah·no

For a guide to pronunciation symbols, see page vi.

WORD	US PRONUNCIATION	UK PRONUNCIATION
paprika	pa·**pree**·ka	**păp**·ri·ka
pasta	**pah**·sta	**pă**·sta
tomato	to·**mā**·toh	to·**mah**·toh

SOME DIFFERENT COOKING MEASUREMENTS

A dessertspoon is unknown as a unit of measure in the US. (It is the equivalent of two teaspoonfuls.) A cup as a unit of measure is 8 fluid ounces in the US rather than 10 fluid ounces as in the UK. Similarly, a pint is 16 fluid ounces in the US rather than 20 fluid ounces. The US fluid ounce is also slightly larger than the UK fluid ounce.

GROCERIES KNOWN BY DIFFERENT NAMES

In compiling this list of comparisons, I have come across several brand names that are as common as, or more common than, the generic name. I felt that it was essential to include these words. No endorsement is intended—or should be interpreted—by the use of these words.

Grocery Names

US	UK
2% milk	semi-skimmed milk
beets	beetroot
biscuit	scone
brown sugar +	demerara sugar [dĕ·mə·**rair**·rə]
candy apple/caramel apple	toffee apple
chocolate-chip cookie	chocolate-chip biscuit

For a guide to pronunciation symbols and other signs, see page vi.

US	UK
cilantro	coriander
cocktail wiener	cheerio
confectioners' sugar (4x powdered)	castor sugar
confectioners' sugar (10x powdered)	icing sugar
cookie	biscuit
corn	sweet corn
corned beef	salt beef
cornstarch	corn flour
cotton candy	candyfloss
crawfish	crayfish +
Cream of Wheat (brand name)	semolina
cured ham	gammon
eggnog +	egg flip
eggplant	aubergine [**oh**·ber·zheen]
endive	chicory
fava bean [**fah**·və]	broad bean
fish stick	fish finger
French fries/fries	chips
garbanzo bean	chickpea
ginger snap	ginger nut
graham cracker	digestive biscuit (similar to a graham cracker)
granola	muesli
green onion/scallion	spring onion
green plum	greengage
ground meat	minced meat
half-and-half	cream (single) +
hamburger +	beefburger

US	UK
hamburger bun	bap
heavy/whipping cream	double cream
heel (on the end of a loaf)	crust
hot dog (without the bun)	frankfurter +
hot dog roll	bridge-roll
Jell-O (brand name)	jelly
jelly/jam	jam
jerky	strips of dried meat
jelly roll	swiss roll
large zucchini	marrow
layer cake	sandwich cake
lima bean [līma]	butter bean
liverwurst	liver sausage
molasses	treacle
oatmeal	porridge
pancake syrup	golden syrup (similar to pancake syrup)
patty	rissole
pickle (dill or sweet)	pickled gherkin
plum pudding +	Christmas pudding
pole bean	stick bean
Popsicle (brand name)	ice lolly
potato chips	crisps
pound cake	Madeira cake
roast +	joint
romaine lettuce	cos lettuce
rutabaga [**roo**·ta·bā·gə]	swede
seed/pit (in fruit)	pip/stone

US	UK
self-rising flour	self-raising flour
sherbet	sorbet [**sor**·bay] +
shrimp +	prawns
smoked herring	kipper
snow peas +	mange-tout [**mahnzh**·too]
soda	fizzy drink/pop +
soda cracker	water biscuit
soybean	soya bean
stick candy	rock +/seaside rock
string bean	runner bean
sucker	lollipop +
Toll House cookie (brand name)	chocolate-chip biscuit
turnip greens	turnip-tops
Vienna sausage	chipolata
white or golden raisin	sultana
wiener [**wee**·ner]	frankfurter +
zucchini [zoo·**kee**·nee]	courgette [cor·**zhet**]

Squash in Britain is an orange or lemon drink made from mixing a concentrate with water. *Sherbet* is a sweet white powder, mainly eaten by children. A *rasher* means a slice of bacon. A *chipolata* is a small sausage. Curiously the dish *macaroni and cheese* in the US is known as *macaroni cheese* in the UK, but *rum raisin* ice cream is known as *rum and raisin* ice cream in the UK. There are some British foods that are not eaten in the US. One example is Marmite, a dark, salty vegetable extract with the consistency of peanut butter that is used as a spread. Vegemite is the equivalent in Australia and New Zealand.

CLOTHING AND SHOES KNOWN
BY DIFFERENT NAMES

When looking for a specific items in a clothing store, you should note that many articles of clothing have different names in the UK and the US. In some cases, the difference in terminology might even lead to a good deal of confusion. Note that *jumper, knickers, suspenders,* and *vest* have very different meanings in the UK and the US.

Clothing and Shoes

US	UK
ascot	cravat
beaded (dress)	diamanté
business suit +	lounge suit
canvas sneakers	plimsolls/pumps
collar stay	collar stiffener
coveralls	boiler suit
crew neck	turtle-neck
cuffs	turn-ups
derby	bowler hat
fedora	trilby
garters	suspenders
golfing knickers	plus-fours +
hose	stockings +
inseam	inside leg
jumper	pinafore dress
knee-highs	pop socks
knickers	knickerbockers
made-to-order	bespoke

US	UK
nightgown	nightdress
off-the-rack	off the peg
oxfords	brogues
pantsuit	trouser suit
panties	knickers
pants +	trousers +
pantyhose	tights
parka +	anorak
pumps (for women)	court shoes
raincoat +	mac/mackintosh
rubber boots +	Wellingtons
ski mask	Balaclava
snaps (fasteners)	press-studs
sneakers	trainers
spike heels	stiletto heels +
sport coat	sports jacket
suspenders	braces
sweater +	woolly/jumper
sweater set	twin set +
turtleneck	polo-neck
tuxedo	dinner jacket
undershirt	vest
undershorts/Jockey shorts	underpants/Y-fronts
vest	waistcoat

SCHOOLS

The British School System

In Britain there are many types of schools. Children may start in *kindergarten,* also known as *nursery school,* then go on to *primary* or *elementary school.* They then start *junior school* at the age of 7, where they stay until the age of 11 or 12. They may also go to a *preparatory school,* or *prep school.* Prep schools are privately run. They then proceed to their high school, which may be a *grammar school,* a *comprehensive school,* or a *grant-maintained school.*

Many *grammar schools* were founded as far back as the sixteenth century. Shakespeare went to a grammar school. In most towns grammar schools were abolished in the 1970s, being considered elitist because prospective students were required to take an entrance exam at age 11 called the 11-plus. A few grammar schools have survived, however, and remain very popular. *Comprehensive schools* (often just called secondary schools) divide pupils of differing abilities into *sets. Grant-maintained schools* are fairly uncommon and are funded by private grants and by the Department for Education. Schools funded by the government are known as *state schools.*

Public schools are elite high schools (often single sex), and are usually very expensive, contrary to what their name implies, although free scholarships are awarded for academic merit. The most famous public schools are Eton and Harrow. Pupils usually attend a prep (preparatory) school before going to a public school.

The school years are designated by *classes* up to high school, and then by *forms.* The highest level of schooling is the sixth form. The school principal is known as the *headmaster.* The school year is divided into three *terms.* A recess is called a *break.* A *tuck shop* sells drinks and snacks.

GCSE exams are taken at the age of 15 or 16, and A-levels, which are required to enter a university, are taken at the age of 17 or 18. GCSE stands for General Certificate of Secondary Education.

Fees are required to attend universities in Britain (but not Scotland), although scholarships are available. Measures of excellence for university degrees are as follows: *first, upper second, lower second,* and *third.* Students who go on for their master's or doctorate are called *postgraduate* students.

The American School System

Just as in Britain, children start in kindergarten or pre-school, if their parents so choose. This is often referred to as K, when speaking of the grade. The children start school proper (first grade) at five or six years of age. This is called *elementary, grammar,* or *grade school.* In elementary school, younger children are encouraged to bring along to school items of interest, e.g., a caterpillar or butterfly, to show the other children. This is called *show and tell.*

Many children take advantage of the free school buses. During the school year, urban roads are fairly swarming with these yellow buses. Other drivers are required to stop behind *and in front* of the bus when it stops to pick up or drop off children, so this can slow down your commute if you get stuck behind one. In the morning many school children are required to recite the *pledge of allegiance.* Prayers are not permitted in public schools; however, some schools have a moment of silence for quiet reflection at the start of the day. The school day starts early and finishes early, sometimes by early afternoon. A late student is given a *tardy slip.* A break is known as a *recess.* There are private schools and *academies,* some of which resemble the British public schools. Universities and colleges are not free, but scholarships are available for some students. Americans call any learning establishment *school,* which can be confusing to Britons. The academic year is usually divided into two terms called *semesters.*

Pupils (often called *students*) normally progress a grade each year, but if they fail their exams (*get a failing grade*), then their GPA (*grade point average*) is not high enough and they must repeat a grade. After grammar school or elementary school, students attend either middle school or junior high school, depending on the system in use in their community. Middle schools start at grade six, and junior high schools at grade seven. Students enter high school at grade nine.

High school graduation is a big event for American school children. It is marked with a ceremony and is an important rite of passage for young adults. There is also a *prom,* or formal dance, in the senior year. At the successful completion of high school, students receive a *high school diploma,* which is required for further study at the university level. The SAT (Scholastic Assessment Test, which was known for many years as the Scholastic Aptitude Test) is the equivalent of A-levels. In high school and college (university), the first-year students are called freshmen, the second-year, sophomores, the third-year, juniors, and the fourth-year, seniors. The head administrator in an elementary or high school is known as the *principal.* A *letter jacket* is a windcheater style of jacket with the initial or initials of a school or college on the front.

The word *student,* which in British English is reserved for those studying at universities, is used in a broader sense in the US and covers anyone studying. An unexpected test in the US is called a *pop quiz.* In the US, if pupils skip a class they *play hookey* or *cut a class.* In the UK, they *skive off.* The expressions *to bunk off* and *play hookey* are known in both countries.

Measures of excellence for US university degrees are as follows: *cum laude, magna cum laude, summa cum laude* (*summa cum laude* being the highest).

Comparison of University Terms

Terms relating to university education are very different, as students from the US or the UK will discover if they decide to study abroad.

University Terms

US	UK
assistant professor	lecturer
associate professor	senior lecturer/reader
commencement	graduation
dormitory	hall of residence
freshman	fresher
full professor	professor
graduate student	postgraduate student
instructor	junior lecturer
major in (a subject)	read (a subject)
proctor	invigilator
president	vice-chancellor
review	revise

In the US, a *frat house* is a residential house for members of a *fraternity*. This is a social organization of male students. The names of fraternities are composed of Greek letters. The equivalent organization for female students is called a *sorority*. Fraternities and sororities sometimes have secret rites, and one must take a pledge to belong. In the US the term *college* is often used interchangeably with *university*. *College* is usually restricted to other forms of higher education in the UK, such as professional or vocational schools.

HEALTH CARE

The British National Health Service does take care of its citizens from cradle to grave, but a patient may have to wait several months, or even years, for a non-emergency operation. British hospitals where the treatment is free are more austere than American hospitals. Emergency treatment is almost invariably undertaken in public hospitals, and ambulances, which are free in an emergency, will take you to one of these. Private hospitals tend to be used for minor surgery or for convalescing. The same doctors (*consultants*) often work in both the private and public sectors, so do not assume that the qualifications or experience of a surgeon or anaesthetist will be better at a private hospital. There are, however, many more trainee or junior doctors working in the public hospitals. The facilities at a private hospital are of course much better, offering the patient a private room, and the nursing staff may be less busy and so able to provide better attention. Perhaps most importantly, you have the ability to choose the day for your operation and avoid long waiting lists.

There is no national health system in the US, but health care is available to all. It is excellent, though very expensive. Those without insurance may have monthly payments to a hospital for many years. Senior citizens are eligible for Medicare, a government health insurance program. The Medicaid program gives health coverage to those with low incomes.

THE POLITICAL SYSTEMS

The US Political System

Legislative bills are presented to the President after being passed by Congress. He has the option of signing the bills into law or vetoing them. If he lets a bill sit on his desk for ten days (excluding Sundays and legal holidays) without either signing it or vetoing it, the bill automatically becomes law. The President is head of the military and also head of state. His term lasts for four years. Legislation must be approved by Congress before it reaches the President's desk to be signed into law or vetoed. Congress consists of two governing bodies, the House of Representatives and the Senate. Each state has two senators, but the number of representatives is proportional to that particular state's population. The House of Representatives is often called *the House*.

The two main parties are the Republicans and the Democrats, which can be compared to the Conservative and Labour parties respectively. The Republicans are often called the GOP (Grand Old Party). The two parties are depicted in cartoons by an elephant and a donkey. The elephant represents the Republicans and the donkey represents the Democrats. When members of a legislative body get together to decide policy, this meeting is known as a *caucus*. A *plurality* occurs when the winning party has more votes than the other parties, but not a majority. In the US a candidate *runs* for office.

The UK Political System

The UK has a parliamentary system of government. A Member of Parliament is often called an MP. (In the US an MP is a military policeman.) There are two houses, the House of Lords and the House of Commons, somewhat like the US Congress. The House of Lords used to consist of *peers,* men and women who belonged to the hereditary nobility or who had been *raised to the peerage,* which means they had been granted the title through merit. People with a title are collectively known as the *peerage.* The House of Lords has now changed with a supposedly more democratic mix of members. The House of Commons consists of elected members who represent their constituency. A *constituency* can mean a district in Britain as well as a body of voters. A candidate *stands* for office in the UK. The three main parties are the Conservative Party, the Labour Party, and the Liberal Democrats. Historically the Conservative Party is right-wing, the Labour Party left-wing. The Conservatives are also called Tories. The leader of the ruling party is known as the Prime Minister.

Britain also elects European members of Parliament known as MEPs (Members of the European Parliament). These represent British interests at the European Parliament in Brussels, Belgium.

MUSEUMS

There are quite a few differences in pronunciation of terms heard in museums and art galleries. A mat around a picture is called a *mount* in the UK. Museum guides are sometimes called *docents* in the US. Here is a list of words often encountered or used in museums that are pronounced differently in the UK and the US.

Pronunciation of Art Historical Terms

WORD	US PRONUNCIATION	UK PRONUNCIATION
baroque	ba·**rōk**	ba·**rŏk**
Byzantine	**biz**·ən·teen	bi·**zan**·tīn
cloche	clōsh	clŏsh
dynasty	**dīn**·as·tee	**dĭn**·as·tee
Huguenot	**hyoo**·gə·not	**hyoo**·gə·noh
Marie Antoinette	mə·**ree** ahn·twa·**net**	**mah**·ree ăn·twa·**net**
Renaissance	**re**·na·sahns	re·**nay**·sens
Van Gogh	van **goh**	van **gof**

For a guide to pronunciation symbols, see page vi.

THE THEATRE

You may wish to take in a show if you are spending time in a big city. The seating is known by different names, so don't be surprised if you are asked if you would like seats in the *orchestra* in the US! They are referring to the seats at the front. If a play *bombs* in the US, it has not gone down well—quite the opposite meaning of the British expression *It went like a bomb,* meaning the play was a hit. The program is sometimes called a *playbill* in the US. The break between acts when the audience may leave their seats to socialize or have a drink is known as *the intermission,* or just *intermission* (without the article) in the US. It is called *the*

46

interval in Britain, where the bar in the theatre is known as a *crush bar,* for obvious reasons. The alternative US spelling *theater* is no longer as common as it used to be. The following conversion chart for theatre terms may be helpful.

Theatre Terms

US	UK
orchestra	stalls
mezzanine	circle
balcony	upper circle/balcony
top balcony	gallery
the peanut gallery	the gods

⫷ 6 ⫸

Differences in Customs and Etiquette

This is a difficult topic to sum up in one chapter, so I've selected some of the cultural differences that I find the most striking. The United States is a melting pot of nationalities. English may be the national language of the US, but many Americans have African, Asian, or Native American ancestors, or ancestors who came from other countries in Europe besides the United Kingdom. While we share the same language to a point, American culture is quite different from that of the UK. Americans use different body language, interact differently with others, and have different customs. Americans will strike up a conversation with a stranger much more readily than a Briton may be accustomed to, and an American may ask questions that a British person could find a little forward. They often terminate even a brief chat with "Well, it was nice talking to (with) you!" or "Have a nice day now!" Friends and acquaintances greet each other with "Hi" or "Hi there" or "How's it going?" Most Americans answer their phone by just saying "Hello," whereas most Britons give their name or phone number. On terminating a telephone conversation, an American might say "Well, I'll let you go now," rather than being blunt and saying "I have to go now." Americans often give a parting pleasantry, such as "Drive safely" or "Enjoy" that may seem rather like a command to a Briton.

"Thank you" always requires a response in the US. The most common response is "You're welcome." In a casual situation you may hear "You bet" or "Uh-huh." A Briton might respond with "Thanks very much," "Not at all," or perhaps "Cheers" in a casual situation. (Most Americans would find this use of the expression "Cheers" very odd, as it is usually used as a toast before drinking in the US.) Sometimes a nod of acknowledgment is considered sufficient response. "Sir" or "Ma'am" is used far more in the US than in Britain. You will hear it often when being served in a restaurant or in other businesses that provide services. It is also used to catch someone's attention, as in "Sir, you left your keys behind." If an American does not understand you, he or she may simply say "Sir?" or "Ma'am?" This means they want you to repeat your statement or "to run that by them one more time." If you are addressed as "Buster" or "Lady," it is probably not too friendly a form of address, and you have most likely offended the person.

As Henry Higgins put it in *My Fair Lady* by Frederick Loewe and Alan Jay Lerner, "An Englishman's way of speaking absolutely classifies him." In the US, the social pecking order is not always as apparent merely by accent as it is in the UK. However, differences between the accents of various social groups in the US can be heard, even by Britons unfamiliar with American dialects, especially in the large cities of the East.

Americans are more inclined to attend church regularly than Britons. An estimated 100 million Americans attend a church every Sunday. Synagogues, also called *temples,* are also well attended.

Drive-ins and drive-through services are popular in the US, especially with banks and fast-food restaurants, although drive-in movies have decreased in numbers since the 1980s. *The soda fountain* (beverage counter) in the local *drugstore* (general store) has all but disappeared. Until the 1960s, the soda fountain was a local meeting place for youngsters in small towns.

Most utility bills (water, electricity, phone, etc.) come

monthly in the US. They often come quarterly (every three months) in Britain, which can give one quite a surprise! Screens on the windows, central heating, and air conditioning are the norm in houses in the southern US. Screens are not found on British windows, and although air conditioning is now common in British cars, private homes, almost without exception, do not have air conditioning. Almost all American cars have air conditioning, automatic transmission, and cruise control. Top-notch American hotels and restaurants, especially in big cities, often provide valet parking. It is customary to leave a small tip when your car is returned.

The United States also has its share of legends and folktales. Americans have Bigfoot, the British have the Loch Ness monster. Bigfoot, otherwise known as Sasquatch, is a large hairy humanoid creature that is said to roam wilderness areas of the US, in particular the Pacific Northwest. From time to time people report sightings of this creature or traces of his enormous footprints.

Foods and eating habits also differ. These differences are covered in the section describing restaurants on page 23.

AMERICAN SPORTS

Baseball is the national summer sport. It is played in a *ballpark,* which consists of an *infield* or *diamond* with the bases, and an *outfield* beyond that area. A person who bats both left-handed and right-handed is known as a *switch hitter.* The word *pitch* is unknown in the US for a playing field. The person who throws the baseball, however, is known as the *pitcher.* The *World Series* in baseball is similar to a *test match* in cricket. Many baseball expressions have made their way into everyday speech. These are listed in this book under Common Metaphorical Baseball Terms, page 125. Baseball players earn huge sums of money, as do football players. Soccer has become increasingly popular in the US recently. Ice hockey (usually just referred to as hockey) is also popular, and of course football (American-style) is a national passion. Fans tend to be reasonably well-behaved and rarely get out of control. Football is played on a *gridiron*, presumably because of the appearance of the white lines on the field. The players wear helmets and lots of padding. American football was modeled on the British game of rugby football. Curiously the term *downfield*, which means deep in the opponents' part of the field, is known as *upfield* in the UK. A *marquee player* is a top player, who draws plenty of fans.

BRITISH SPORTS

Football in Britain is synonymous with soccer. American football is slowly gaining acceptance in and around London. The padding worn by the players is somewhat amusing to the Brits, who can sustain nasty injuries in their games with little body protection. *Rugger*, or rugby football, is closer to American football, where you can run with the ball. A sporting event is called a *fixture* in Britain, and a *playing field* is also called a *pitch*.

Tennis terms are quite different in Britain. One calls *rough or smooth* to determine the server rather than *up or down*. The *toss* is frequently called the *throw up* in Britain. The call is *van in* rather than *ad in* after deuce, and before play one has a *knock-up* instead of a *warm-up*. If the ball falls in the *alley* it is said to have fallen in the *tramlines* in Britain. The terms *fifteen up*, meaning *fifteen apiece*, and *all tied up*, meaning the players are *tied*, are only used in the US. In American English, *Australian doubles* or *Canadian doubles* is a tennis game for three players.

Cricket is the big summer game in Britain. There are a few cricket terms used in everyday speech in Britain. Throwing the cricket ball is called *bowling*, and the expression *Well bowled!* means *Well done!* To be *on a good wicket* means to be in a good position. To be *on a sticky wicket* is not so good. *Knocked for six* means *thrown for a loop*. To *bowl a googly* means to throw a curve ball. Teams played cricket on a regular basis in Central Park, New York, years ago, but now baseball has taken over.

PUBLIC HOLIDAYS

In Britain, the *bank holidays* include New Year's Day, Good Friday, Easter Monday, and May Day, which honors workers, on the first Monday in May. The Spring Holiday occurs on the last Monday in May. There is also the August Bank Holiday, occurring on the last Monday in August. After Christmas there is Boxing Day. This is the day after Christmas unless Christmas falls on a Saturday, in which case Boxing Day is celebrated the following Monday. Mothering Sunday occurs on the fourth Sunday in Lent. This is also known as Mother's Day.

In the US, the term *legal holiday* is used instead of *bank holiday*. Legal holidays include New Year's Day, Martin Luther King Jr. Day, which occurs on the third Monday in January, Presidents' Day, which occurs on the third Monday in February, and Memorial Day, formerly Decoration Day, which occurs on the last Monday in May and is in remembrance of men and women who were killed in war. Memorial Day is the unofficial beginning of summer. The Fourth of July, also called Independence Day, commemorates the adoption of the Declaration of Independence in 1776. It is celebrated with picnics and later, after sunset, with fireworks. Labor Day, which occurs on the first Monday in September, honors labor and is unofficially considered to mark the end of summer. Columbus Day, the second Monday in October, is celebrated in most states. Veterans' Day is on November 11.

There is a big celebration at Thanksgiving, another important US holiday. Thanksgiving occurs on the fourth Thursday in November. Thanksgiving Day, which became a national holiday in 1863, commemorates the first harvest of the Pilgrims in America in 1621. It is traditionally celebrated with turkey and pumpkin pie and is a time of family get-togethers and much feasting. Travel arrangements must be made well in advance if you wish to travel at this time. Christmas decorations usually appear in the shops around this time and sometimes even before.

The American flag is seen flying everywhere all year round, from outside post offices to on the backs of motorcycles. Flags must be illuminated at night or be taken down. Groundhog Day occurs on February 2. According to legend, if the groundhog emerges from hibernation on this day and sees its shadow, there will be another six weeks of winter weather. Mother's Day occurs on the second Sunday in May.

Paid *vacations* (*holidays* in the UK) are more generous in Britain on the whole.

⊰ 7 ⊱

Transportation

Terminology used in vehicles and on the roads is very different in the two countries. In addition to incorporating some terms while describing driving in the two countries, I have included complete lists of term comparisons at the end of this section.

THE BRITISH ROAD

British roads consist of *B roads, A roads,* and *motorways.* B roads are roughly similar to *state roads* in the US, A roads are similar to *US highways,* and motorways are similar to *US interstates.* Motorways all have the designation M such as the M25. Apart from driving on the other side of the road, there are several other important differences between the UK and the US in the rules of the road. Traffic lights go from red to combined red and amber before turning green. This alerts the driver that the light is about to turn green. Pedestrian crossings with a traffic light are known as *pelican crossings,* from *pe*destrian *li*ght *con*trolled crossing. After red, the traffic light will go to a flashing amber light, which means that pedestrians have the right of way, but the cars may proceed if no one is on the crossing. The traffic light will then turn green. A round sign on a pole with a black diagonal stripe on a white background indicates the end of a speed restriction.

The maximum speed in Britain is 70 miles per hour. Seat belts must be worn in both front and rear seats. Signposts do not always give compass directions, so it is advisable to consult the map and note towns and cities through which you will be traveling for reference. It is prohibited to overtake from a slower lane. *Yield* signs say *Give Way.*

The signs on motorways are blue and are very similar to the signs on US interstates. Signs on other roads have black lettering on white or yellow on green. The ramps on and off the motorways are known as *slip roads.* Emergency telephones at one mile intervals are common on the motorways. Traffic circles are known as *roundabouts* and are very common in Britain. Usually the traffic on the roundabout has priority over traffic entering. A traffic back-up is frequently called a *tailback.* A sign saying *ramp* indicates there is a difference in the level of the road surface ahead, usually because of construction.

A divided highway is called a *dual carriageway,* and the median is known as the *central reservation.* A green arrow is often called a *filter.*

In the UK, lorries (called *trucks* in the US) with a cab and a trailer are known as *articulated lorries.* Signs often use the term *HGV* (*Heavy Goods Vehicle*) or *LGV* (*Large Goods Vehicle*) when referring to them. The term *LGV* was supposed to replace *HGV* in 1992, but now both abbreviations are used interchangeably.

THE AMERICAN ROAD

The *interstates* are the equivalent of the British motorways. The slip roads are called *on ramps* and *off ramps.* Emergency telephones on the interstates are rather sporadic. Sometimes they are at one-mile intervals, but very often you can go miles without seeing one.

The US equivalent of the British A and B roads are the US and SR roads. The US stands, of course, for United States, the SR for state road. The only difference between these roads is that the US roads continue from one state into the next, whereas the SR roads will only take you within the state you are in and are given a different number in the next state. C roads, or county roads, tend to have only one lane in each direction and usually are rural. Unlike the British, Americans never use the article with roads. They say, "Take US 27 north," rather than "Take *the* US 27 north."

The center of the US road is marked with yellow lines; white lines are used as lane dividers. In many urban areas over the last 20 years, the *median* or *median strip* (known as the *central reservation* in Britain) has been made into a turn lane. This keeps the fast lane moving, although occasionally two cars from opposite directions will meet in the middle lane, blocking each other's view. A word of caution here: sometimes the right (slow) lane turns into a right-turn-only lane, with very little warning, necessitating a fast lane change if you don't want to turn. Overtaking (*passing* in the US) is permitted from a slower lane.

If you encounter a school bus that has stopped to pick up or set down children, you *must* stop if you are behind the bus and also if you are approaching the bus from the other direction when on a road without a central reservation.

Most towns and cities are laid out in a grid pattern. Thus in some cities or towns, avenues will intersect streets, while in others, numbered streets will intersect named streets with avenues running diagonally through the city. Yet no matter what the variation, there is usually a consistent north-south or east-west direction to all thoroughfares. Accordingly, street addresses are thereby simplified; for example, 2903 14th Street West will be very close to the corner of 29th Avenue and 14th Street West. The giving of directions is also simplified by this method. One might say, "Go north along 26th Street, turn right at the third light, go two blocks, then turn left"; or one could be more specific and say, "Go north along 26th street, turn east at 39th Avenue, then north at 19th Street." A *block* is often used for measuring distances in a city. It means the distance between intersecting streets. Even in the country one might hear the term *city block* used as a measurement.

The term *street* in the US is not restricted to urban areas as it is in Britain. The American equivalent of the British *high street* is *main street.*

In urban areas, almost every set of traffic lights will include turning arrows that allow for left turns before oncoming traffic proceeds. Traffic lights are also known as stop lights, red lights, or lights. One set of lights is known simply as a *light,* e.g. "Turn at the next light" or "This is a long light." The *amber light* is known as the *yellow light* in the US. Almost everywhere in the US you can turn right at a traffic light, even if it is red, unless otherwise indicated. You must, of course, stop first to see if it is safe to proceed. In fact, if you are sitting at a traffic light in the right lane with your right turn signal flashing, the car behind you may become impatient if you make no attempt to turn. Sometimes you may see a sign that says "No turn on red"; then, of course, you must wait for the light to turn green. This system had been used in certain states for many years, but after the oil crisis in 1973 making a right turn on a red light became almost universal as a means of reducing fuel consumption.

Each state has its own driver's license. This is the size of a credit card and has the bearer's photograph on the front. These cards are commonly used for identification purposes, especially when cashing a check or entering a bar. Some states only require one number-plate, called a *license plate* in the US, at the rear of the car.

INTERSTATE DRIVING

Driving on the interstates is very similar to driving on the motorways. The interstate signs are shaped like a blue shield with the road number, such as I-95 or I-4, written in white letters inside the shield. In Hawaii the letter H is used instead of

I to indicate an interstate, e.g. H-2. In Alaska they use an A. The even-numbered interstates run east to west with the lower numbers in the extreme south of the United States and the highest numbers in the north. The odd-numbered interstates run north to south, with the lowest numbers in Hawaii (H-1) and the highest numbers on the eastern seaboard of the continental US. Spur roads and orbital roads around large cities are designated by three-digit numbers. Spur road numbers will start with an odd digit, e.g. I-395. Roads, such as bypasses, that link up with main roads at each end will start with an even number, e.g. I-295. Alaska has four interstate highways, A-1 through A-4. Even though these Alaskan routes are designated as interstate highways, they are generally not constructed to Interstate standards and marked as Alaska State Routes. The interstates have rather infrequent rest areas, which usually consist of toilets (restrooms), vending machines, and tables and chairs for picnics. They are generally quite attractive but rarely sell gasoline (petrol) or hot food as do the *services* in Britain. On some toll roads or turnpikes you will find rest areas with full services. Quite often these are located in the center of the road (on a large road divider), necessitating an exit from the fast lane. The fastest speed at which you may travel on the interstates varies from state to state. Occasionally a slip road will lead into the fast lane, which will require your quickly having to attain the speed of the other traffic. The slow lane in the US is known as the *outside* lane; quite the opposite of the slow lane in Britain which is known as the *inside* lane. The reason for the opposite term being used has apparently nothing to do with the fact that the two countries drive on different sides of the road. In South Africa, where left-hand rule applies (where you drive on the left), the slow lane is known as the outside line.

Speed limits in the US are observed quite well, mainly because the police are very vigilant. The highway police of the respective states through which the interstates run patrol these roads (sometimes from the air). These highway patrol officers are also known as *state troopers*.

Each state has counties, much like British counties. County roads outside the city limits are patrolled by *deputy sheriffs* (known commonly as *deputies* or *sheriffs*), urban areas by the city police. In some states there are also *state police*. If you have ever wondered where the word *Smokey* came from, here's the story: Smokey Bear was introduced on a poster by the National Forest Service in 1944 as part of a campaign to educate the public on fire prevention in forests and parks. The bear's big hat resembled that of the state troopers, and soon truckers were referring to a state trooper, or any traffic patrol officer, as a Smokey.

In the US, *articulated lorries* are called *tractor-trailers*. The more common term for a large rig is an *eighteen-wheeler* or *semi* [**sem·ī**]. As they travel the interstates, they are sporadically required to pull in at *weigh stations* in each state to be weighed. This is for safety reasons, since an overloaded truck could be a menace on the roads.

RULES OF THE ROAD

Have you ever wondered why Americans drive on the right? Peter Kincaid has written an excellent book on the subject entitled *The Rule of the Road* (Greenwood Press, 1986). He thinks that right-hand rule probably goes back to the early wagons used in the US, where the driver either walked on the left side of the animals that pulled the wagon, or rode on the left rear animal. The reason for this is that most people are right-handed, mount a horse from the left, and prefer to lead a horse with their right hand. Because of this, the early travelers preferred to keep right so that they could more accurately judge the clearance between passing vehicles. In Britain, wagons were mostly driven from the box with the driver seated on the right so that he could use the brake and whip with his right hand. Mounting posts for horses in the UK were situated on the left side of streets, as horses are mounted from the left side. This resulted in a preference for a keep-left rule in Britain. No doubt European settlers also influenced drivers in the US to keep right; and with the arrival of the automobile at the beginning of the twentieth century, the same rules were followed. Curiously, the early American cars had right-hand drive to help the driver see the deep ditches at the sides of the poorly maintained roads, and perhaps to facilitate entering and exiting the car. Interestingly, John McAdam, the inventor of tarmac, constructed a highway that used the left-hand rule until the mid-1800s. It was called the National Pike or the Cumberland Road and ran from Cumberland, Maryland, inland toward Saint Louis, Missouri. It is now known as US 40.

TERMS FOR THE ROAD (UK–US)

This section treats terms relating to automobiles and roads which are particular to either the UK or the US. In compiling this lexicon I have come across several brand names that are as common as, or more common than, the generic name. Because the brand names may not be understood in the other country, I found it essential to include these words.

British Car Terminology

UK	US
accident +	wreck
articulated lorry	semi [**sem**·ī]/tractor-trailer/eighteen-wheeler
black spot	dangerous stretch of road
bollard*	traffic diverter
bonnet	hood
boot	trunk
bull bar/bullbar	grill/bumper guard
camper van/Caravanette (brand name)	conversion van

For a guide to pronunciation symbols and other signs, see page vi.

UK	US
car park	parking lot
caravan	trailer
Cat's-eyes (brand name)	reflectors (on the road)
central reservation	median/median strip
chippings	gravel/small stones
coach	tour bus/motor coach
coupé [**coo**·pay]	coupe [coop]
crash barrier	guardrail
cut up (a driver)	cut off
derv (**d**iesel-**e**ngined **r**oad **v**ehicle)	diesel fuel for trucks
dipped headlights	low-beam headlights
diversion	detour
dog leg (in road)	jog
drink driving	drunk driving
drunk in charge	DUI (driving under the influence)/ DWI (driving while intoxicated)
driving licence	driver's license
dual carriageway	divided highway
estate car	station wagon +
excess (on insurance)	deductible
exhaust pipe +	tailpipe
filter light	green arrow
flat battery	dead battery
flyover	overpass
forecourt (at a filling station)	area around the gas pumps
gear lever	gearshift
give way	yield

UK	US
HGV (heavy goods vehicle)	semi [**sem**·ī]/eighteen-wheeler
hand brake	parking brake +/emergency brake
hoarding	billboard +
indicator	turn signal
juggernaut	eighteen-wheeler
jump leads	jumper cables
lay-by	pull-off/turnout (seldom found in US)
lorry	truck
LGV	semi [**sem**·ī]/eighteen-wheeler
manual transmission +	stick shift/standard transmission
motorway	interstate/freeway
mudguard	fender
multi-storey car park	parking garage/parking ramp (regional North)
nearside lane/inside lane	outside lane (closest to the curb)
number-plate	tag/license plate
offside lane/outside lane	inside lane
on tow	in tow
overtake +	pass +
pantechnicon [pan·**tek**·ni·con]	moving van
pavement	sidewalk
pelican crossing	pedestrian crossing with lights
petrol	gas/gasoline
prang	fender bender
puncture +	flat/flat tire +
ramp	speed bump +
removal van	moving van

UK	US
reverse +	back up
roadworks	road construction/road work
roundabout	traffic circle/rotary (regional New England)
services	service area
sidelights	parking lights
sleeping policeman	speed bump +
slip road	on ramp/off ramp
speed hump	speed bump
speedo	speedometer +
subway	pedestrian underpass
tailback	traffic backup
tailboard	tailgate
tarmac	blacktop
third-party insurance	liability insurance
traffic island	median
traffic lights/traffic light +	red light/stop light/light
traffic warden	parking enforcement officer
transport café	truck stop
unmade road	dirt road
verge	shoulder +/side median
way out	exit +
windscreen	windshield
wing mirror	side-view mirror
zebra crossing	crosswalk/pedestrian crossing +

TERMS FOR THE ROAD (US–UK)

There are also terms used in the US that British visitors to the US may not know or that may not be understood in the UK if an American visitor uses them.

American Car Terminology

US	UK
antique car (See definition at the end of this section.)	vintage car
automobile/auto (rarely spoken)	car +
back up	reverse +
barrel along *(colloq.)*	belt along
bias-ply tires	cross-ply tyres
billboard +	hoarding
blacktop	tarmac
body man	panel beater
boot (wheel immobilizer)	wheel clamp
break in (engine)	run in
brights/bright lights	main beams
bumper guard	overrider or bullbar (The type is specified in the UK.)
carburetor [**kar**·bur·ay·tor]	carburettor [kar·**bur**·ĕ·tor]
cattle guard	cattle grid
conversion van	camper van
coupe [coop]	coupé [**coo**·pay]
crosswalk	zebra crossing/pedestrian crossing +
cruiser	police car +
cut off (someone)	cut up
dead battery	flat battery

For a guide to pronunciation symbols and other signs, see page vi.

US	UK
deadhead *(verb)*	drive without a load
deductible (on insurance)	excess
defogger	demister
detail (clean a car thoroughly)	valet
detour	diversion
dimmer switch	dip switch
dirt road	unmade road
divided highway	dual carriageway
double clutch	double declutch
drive shaft	prop shaft
driver's handbook	highway code
driver's license	driving licence
DUI (driving under the influence)/ DWI (driving while intoxicated)	drink driving
dump truck	tipper truck
emergency brake	hand brake/parking brake +
exit +	way out
fender	wing/mudguard
fender bender	minor traffic accident
fender skirt	wheel spat
flat/flat tire +	puncture +
four-lane highway/four lane	dual carriageway
freeway	motorway
freeze plug	core plug +
gas/gasoline	petrol
gas mileage	fuel consumption +
gas pedal	accelerator
gearshift	gear lever
grease fitting	grease nipple

US	UK
grille guard	bullbar
guardrail	crash barrier
hairpin curve/turn	hairpin bend
half shaft	drive shaft
headliner	headlining
high-beam headlights	main-beam headlights
high gear	top gear
hitch	tow bar
hood	bonnet
hood ornament	mascot
in tow	on tow
inside lane	offside lane/outside lane
interstate	motorway
jog (in road)	dogleg
jumper cables	jump leads
lemon (car)	dud/Friday-afternoon car
liability insurance	third-party insurance
license plate	number-plate
low-beam headlights	dipped headlights
low gear	bottom gear/first gear +
lug nut	wheel nut
make/hang a right (left)	turn right (left) +
median/median strip	central reservation/island
minivan	people carrier
motor home	Caravanette (brand name)
moving van	removal van
mudguard	mudflap +
muffler	silencer

US	UK
no outlet	no through road +
no standing	no stopping
odometer +	milometer
oil pan	sump
outside lane (slow lane)	nearside lane/inside lane
parking garage/ramp (regional North)	multi-storey car park
parking lights	sidelights
parking lot	car park
parkway	tree-lined dual carriageway
patrolman	police officer
pavement	road surface
ping (engine sound)	pink
RV (recreational vehicle)	Caravanette (brand name)
rear-ended	hit by the car behind
red light	traffic light
reflectors (on the road)	Cat's-eyes (brand name)
rest area	lay-by/services
restroom	toilet/lavatory
rotary (regional New England)	roundabout
rumble seat	dickey seat
sedan	saloon
semi [sem·ī]	articulated lorry/HGV/LGV
shop	repair shop
side median	verge
side mirror/side-view mirror	wing mirror
sidewalk	pavement/footpath
Smokey (slang)	highway patrol officer

US	UK
spark-plug wires	spark-plug leads
standard transmission	manual transmission +
station wagon +	estate car
stick shift	manual transmission +
stoplight	traffic light +
striping the pavement	white-lining the road
tag (regional)	registration sticker/number-plate
tailgate +	tailboard
tailgate (verb)	drive on someone's tail
totaled, was	is a write-off (expressed differently in each country)
traffic circle	roundabout
trailer	caravan
trailer hitch	tow-bar
transmission +	gearbox
trooper	highway patrol officer
truck	lorry/pick-up
trunk	boot
turning radius	turning circle
turnout (regional West)	lay-by
two-cycle engine	two-stroke engine
valve cover	rocker cover
vehicle inspection certificate	MOT (Ministry of Transport) certificate
vent window	quarter light
windshield	windscreen
wreck	accident +
yield +	give way

The term *classic car* is used rather loosely in both countries. However, a car made prior to 1918 is a *veteran car* in the UK, and one made between 1918 and 1930 is known as a *vintage car*. In the US, a car made between 1925 and 1945 is known as a *classic car*. If a car is over 25 years old, it is classified as an *antique car*.

PRONOUNCING CAR NAMES IN THE UK AND US

There are also a few names of car brands and models (including both British-made models and models made elsewhere) that are pronounced differently in the UK and the US, although both Americans and Britons will be familiar with the written forms of the names. In addition, a BMW car in the US is often affectionately called a *Beamer* or *Bimmer,* and a Mercedes in Britain is sometimes called a *Merc.*

British Pronunciations of Car Names

BRAND OR MODEL NAME	UK PRONUNCIATION
Daimler	**dām**·lə
Datsun	**dăt**·**sun**
Fiat	**fee**·ăt
Jaguar	**jag**·yu·ah
Mazda	**măz**·da
Mondeo	mon·**day**·oh
Nissan	**nis**·ən
Peugeot	**per**·zhoh
Renault	**ren**·oh
Vauxhall	**vox**·all

For a guide to pronunciation symbols and other signs, see page vi.

American Pronunciations of Car Names

BRAND OR MODEL NAME	US PRONUNCIATION
Bonneville	**bon**·ə·vil
Brougham	brome
Chevrolet	**shev**·ro·lay
Chrysler	**krīs**·ler
Ciera	see·**air**·ra
Daimler	**dīm**·ler
Datsun	**daht**·sun
DeVille	duh·**vil**
Fiat	**fee**·aht
Galant	ga·**lahnt**
Grand Prix	grand pree
Hyundai	**hun**·day
Jaguar	**jag**·war
Marquis	mar·**kee**
Mazda	**mahz**·da
Miata	mee·**ah**·ta
Nissan	**nee**·sahn
Peugeot	pyoo·**zhoh**
Renault	re·**nawlt**

For a guide to pronunciation symbols and other signs, see page vi.

RAILROAD (RAILWAY) TERMS

There are a few differences in terminology relating to the railroad, or as they are called in the UK, the railway. The term *railroad* itself was once used in the UK, but it was replaced by the term *railway* already in the 19th century. *Amtrak* is the name of the American national passenger rail system created by Congress in 1970. The name stands for *American Travel by Track*.

Railroad Terminology

US	UK
boxcar	goods wagon
bumpers	buffers
caboose	guard's van
car	carriage
coach (class of travel)	second class
conductor	guard
depot [**dee**·poh]	station +
dining car/diner	restaurant car
emergency cord	communication cord
engineer	engine driver
freight car	goods wagon
freight train	goods train
gondola car	truck
grade crossing	level crossing
layover	stopover +
one-way ticket	single ticket
passenger car	carriage
railroad crossing	level crossing
railroad ties	railway sleepers
roundtrip ticket	return ticket
switch *(noun)*	points
switch, to *(verb)*	shunt +
switch tower	signal box
switchyard	shunting yard

For a guide to pronunciation symbols and other signs, see page vi.

US	UK
ticket agent	booking clerk
track 1	platform 1
track layer	platelayer
train station	railway station
trestle	wooden bridge supported by wooden trestles
truck (set of wheels)	bogie
whistle-stop*	halt (similar)

≼ 8 ≽

Pronunciation and Grammar

An Englishman's way of speaking
absolutely classifies him.

HENRY HIGGINS in *My Fair Lady,*
by Frederick Loewe and Alan Jay Lerner

Both Americans and Britons have many regional accents. The linguistic term *accent* refers to a variety of speech distinguished by pronunciation differences, whereas the term *dialect* includes varieties differing in grammar and vocabulary as well as pronunciation.

One important way in which dialects of English often differ is in the pronunciation (or lack of pronunciation) of the consonant *r*. A dialect is called *rhotic* [**roe**·tik] if the *r* is pronounced before a consonant or at the end of a word. (This linguistic term is derived from the name of the Greek letter *rho*.) Similarly, a dialect is called *non-rhotic* when consonant *r* is not pronounced before a consonant or at the end of a word. For example, in the present-day non-rhotic speech of Britain, *harm* sounds something like [hahm] and *farther* and *father* both sound like [**fah**·tha]. The weakening of *r* probably began in Britain in the 1600s, and the *r* began to be lost completely in the middle of

73

the 1700s. Completely *r*-less speech only became standard in Britain in the 1800s. (Note that the *r*'s are kept in British speech at the beginning of words and between vowels. *Rare* is pronounced something like [**ray**·uh], and only the first *r* is pronounced as an *r*; the second makes an *uh* sound, or is dropped entirely. When it is dropped completely, the word sounds something like [reh]. However, *rarer* is pronounced something like [**ray**·rə], and the second *r* is pronounced because it is now between two vowels.)

It is thought that some colonists in New England may have spoken a dialect of English in which the *r*'s were sounded weakly—that is, the dialect was beginning to become *non-rhotic*. The first Pilgrims arrived on the Mayflower in 1620 from Plymouth, England, but many of them were originally from the Midlands and East Anglia. English settlers in North America from these areas may have had weakened *r*'s or non-rhotic speech. In comparison with some other British colonies in North America, New England maintained closer ties with England during the Colonial period. During this period the *r*-less variety of English began to become common in the south of Britain. The continual influence from the British *r*-less standard would have reinforced the possible *r*-weakening tendencies of the original dialects of the Pilgrims, and this explains the non-rhotic speech in the New England area today. The *r*-less dialects in other areas of the United States, such as certain parts in the South, have a similar history.

Other colonists came from the West Country in England and settled further south than New England. They would have spoken with an accent probably not too unlike the present-day accent in the county of Devon, England, which has rhotic speech. Later Scots-Irish immigrants also had rhotic speech. The mixture of many different groups speaking rhotic dialects from Britain and Ireland explains the rhotic speech heard in most of the US today.

Most Britons have been so well exposed to American accents through the media and movies that they have little difficulty understanding the various accents, although some of the Southern accents are hard even for fellow Americans to understand. Americans have a much more difficult time understanding British speech, so if a Briton wants to be understood easily, avoid slang—it is by no means universal—and speak slowly and clearly.

Vowel sounds are quite different. In Britain the vowel sound in such words as *paw, talk,* and *all,* etc., is similar to the sound in *bore* without pronouncing the *r.* In the US, it becomes *ah* in some dialects resulting in [pah], [tahk], and [ahl]. Also the *o* in *hot, top, on,* and so forth is pronounced in British English with rounded lips, quite different from the American sound. In some American dialects, the vowel sound spelled *au* in *caught* and *aw* in *caw* and the vowel sound spelled *o* in *cot* have become the same, as in the names *Don* and *Dawn.* However, Americans distinguish clearly between *talk* and *torque,* which are phonetically the same for British people.

In the US, a *t* is usually pronounced with a sound like *d* when it comes within a word between vowels or after *r* and before a vowel. Hence *thirty, dirty,* and *fruity* may sound like *thirdy, dirdy,* and *fruidy.* Sometimes the *t* is lost altogether in words like *dentist* and *interesting,* which can sound like *dennist* and *inneresting.* The *ai* in *rain* and *stain* is slightly shorter than its British counterpart, as is the *ew* sound in *few* and *grew.* In the US, the short *a* (the vowel in *cat*) is used in *chance* and *fast,* but it is more drawn out than its counterpart in Northern Britain. Words ending with *ary, ory,* and *ery* are not contracted as they are in British speech. Similarly the word *berry,* when forming part of the names of fruits such as *raspberry* and *strawberry,* is not contracted to [bree] in American speech. Americans may pronounce the *o* in words such as *orange* and *Florida* with a short *o* as the British pronounce it, or like the *o* in the word *or.* However, there is much variation as to which vowel is used in which words. In Maine the *or* sound as in *short* sounds like [ah]. Similarly the word *news* may be pronounced [nooz] or [nyooz], although [nooz] is more common. Americans pronounce the *u* in the words *mutual, cube, butane, Cuba,* and *Houston* as a *yoo* sound like the British.

The southern states in the US have an accent distinct from that of the northern states. The most noticeable characteristic is the long *i,* which becomes a drawn-out *ah* sound. For example, the word *wide* sounds like [wahd]. Often the final vowel in a word becomes an indeterminate vowel sound, e.g., *Miami* is sometimes pronounced [my·**am**·ə]. You will frequently hear the expression *y'all* in the South. This is a contraction of *you all* and is frequently used when addressing more than one person. *You-uns* is used in the same way in some areas, such as the Appalachians. Another Southern trait is putting emphasis on the first syllable in words such as *entire* and *insurance.*

In Britain, words such as *tune* and *dual* are sometimes pronounced *choon* and *jewel.* You will often hear an intrusive *r* in phrases such as *saw it* (sounding something like *sore it*) in Britain, but this is rarely heard in the US except in the New England area. *Issue* and *tissue* are sometimes pronounced [**is**·yoo] and [**tis**·yoo]. In the north of England the *u* sound in *putt* is almost the same vowel as in *put,* and *book* may have the vowel sound of *hoot.*

Aluminum is not only pronounced differently, but it is spelled differently in the two countries. Sir Humphrey Davy, who discovered the metal in 1908, called it *aluminum.* It was later changed in Britain to *aluminium* to conform to the spelling and sound of similar elements in the periodic table, such as titanium. However, in the US the old form still exists.

SOME PRONUNCIATION DIFFERENCES

In discussing the differences in pronunciation between British English and American English, I have decided not to use the International Phonetic Alphabet, or IPA, simply because most readers are not familiar with the symbols.

In general, English words that have recently been borrowed from French are pronounced in the US with the emphasis on the last syllable. For example, *consommé* is pronounced [con·**som**·ay] in the UK, but [con·sə·**may**] in the US. The past tenses of the verbs *to dive, to fit,* and *to sneak* are often *dove, fit,* and *snuck* in the US, but in the UK it is *dived, fitted,* and *sneaked.* The past participles of the verbs *to get* and *to mow* are *gotten* and *mowed* respectively in the US, rather than *got* and *mown* as in British English. The past tense of the verb *to plead* may be *pleaded* or *pled* in the US, whereas only *pleaded* is used in the UK.

Here are some common words that differ in pronunciation.

American and British Pronunciations Compared

WORD	US PRONUNCIATION	UK PRONUNCIATION
accent	**ak**·sent	**ak**·sənt
advertisement	ad·ver·**tīz**·ment	ad·**vert**·is·ment
agile	**a**·jəl	**a**·jīl
albino	al·**bīn**·ō	al·**bee**·nō
alternate *(adj., noun)*	**ault**·er·nət	aul·**tern**·et
altimeter	al·**tim**·ə·ter	**al**·ti·mee·ter
amenity	a·**měn**·ə·tee	a·**meen**·ə·tee
anchovy	an·**chō**·vee	**an**·chə·vee
anti	**an**·tī/**an**·tee	**an**·tee
apparatus	ap·a·**ră**·tus	ap·a·**ray**·tus
aristocrat	a·**ris**·to·crat	a·**ris**·to·crat
asphalt	**as**·fault	**as**·felt
ate	āte	ett
ballet	bal·**ay**	**bal**·ay
barrage	bə·**rahzh**	**bă**·rahzh
baton	bə·**tŏn**	**bă**·tŏn
been	bin	been
beta	**bay**·ta	**bee**·ta

For a guide to pronunciation symbols and other signs, see page vi.

WORD	US PRONUNCIATION	UK PRONUNCIATION
bitumen	bī·**too**·men	**bĭ**·cher·men
brassiere	brə·**zeer**	**brăs**·eeə
buoy	**boo**·ee	boy
byzantine	**biz**·an·teen	bi·**zan**·tīn
capillary	**cap**·il·ar·ee	ca·**pil**·ə·ree
caramel	**cahr**·ə·mel	**căr**·ə·mel +
caribbean	kə·**rib**·ē·an	kar·ĭ·**bee**·an +
carillon	**kar**·i·lon	kə·**ril**·yon
charade	sha·**rād**	**sha**·rahd
chassis	**cha**·see	**sha**·see
chimpanzee	chim·**pan**·zee (regional)	chimp·ən·**zee**
clerk	klerk	klark
clientele	clī·en·**tel**	clē·ən·**tel**
cobra	**cō**·bra	**cō**·bra/**cŏ**·bra
combatant	com·**băt**·ant	**com**·bə·tant
composite	kəm·**pŏz**·it	**kŏm**·pə·zit
compost	**com**·pōst	**com**·pŏst
condom	**con**·dəm	**con**·dŏm
conduit	**cŏn**·doo·it	**cŏn**·dit
consommé	con·sə·**may**	con·**som**·ay
contractor	**con**·trac·ter	con·**trac**·ter
controversy	**con**·trə·ver·see +	con·**trŏv**·er·see
cordial	**cor**·jəl	**cor**·dee·al
cremate	**cree**·māte	crə·**māte**
croquet	crō·**kay**	**crō**·kay
cuckoo	**koo**·koo	**kû**·koo
cyclamen	**sīk**·lə·men	**sĭk**·lə·men
dahlia	**dă**·lee·ə	**dā**·lee·ə

WORD	US PRONUNCIATION	UK PRONUNCIATION
debris	də·**bree**	**deb**·ree
dehydrated	de·**hȳ**·drā·ted	de·hy·**drā**·ted
depot	**dee**·pō/**dĕ**·pō	**dĕ**·pō
detail	de·**tail**	**dee**·tail
devolution	dĕ·va·**loo**·shn	dee·va·**loo**·shn
dislocate	dis·**lō**·cate	**dis**·lo·cate +
diverge	dĭ·**verge**	**dī**·verge
docile	**dŏ**·səl	**dō**·sīl
double entendre	**du**·bəl on·**tahn**·dra	**doo**·blə on·**tahn**·dra
dressage	drə·**sahzh**	**dres**·ahzh
dynasty	**dī**·nas·tee	**dĭn**·as·tee
entrepreneur	on·tra·prə·**noor**	on·tra·prə·**ner**
cra	**ĕr**·ə	**ear**·ə
err	air	er
figure	**fig**·yer/**fi**·ger	**fi**·ger
forsythia	for·**sĭth**·ē·a	for·**sīth**·ē·a
fragile	**fra**·jəl	fra·**jīle**
frequent *(verb)*	**free**·kwent	free·**kwent**
frustrate	**frus**·trāt	frus·**trāt**
gala	**gă**·la/**gā**·la	**gah**·la
garage	ga·**rahzh**	**gar**·ij/**gar**·ahzh
geyser	**gī**·zer	**gee**·zer
glacier	**glay**·sher	**glăs**·ē·er
glazier	**glay**·zher	**glay**·zēer
gooseberry	**goos**·bĕ·ree	**gûz**·bə·ree
hoof	**hûf**	**hoof**
hostile	**hos**·təl	**hos**·tīl
hurricane	**hurr**·i·kane	**hur**·ri·kən

WORD	US PRONUNCIATION	UK PRONUNCIATION
idyllic	ī·**dĭll**·ik	ĭ·**dill**·ik
inquiry	**in**·kwĭ·ree/in·**kwīr**·ee	in·**kwīr**·ee
interesting	**in**·ter·est·ing	**in**·trest·ing
iodine	ī·**oh**·dine	ī·**oh**·deen
jaguar	**jag**·wahr	**jag**·u·ah
junta	**hûn**·ta	**jun**·ta
khaki	**kă**·kee	**kah**·kee
laboratory	**lab**·ra·tor·ee	la·**bor**·a·tree
lasso	la·**soh**	las·**oo** +
lavatory	**lav**·ə·taur·ee	**lav**·ə·tree
leisure	**lee**·zhure	**lĕzh**·ure
lever	**lĕv**·er	**leev**·er
lieutenant	loo·**ten**·ant	lef·**ten**·ant
lilac	**lī**·lăk	**lī**·lək
liposuction	**lī**·pō·suk·shən	**lĭ**·pō·suk·shən
literally	**li**·ter·a·lee	**lit**·ra·lee
macho	**mah**·chō	**mă**·chō
mambo	**mahm**·bo	**măm**·bo
marquis	mar·**kee**	**mar**·kwis
mauve	mauv/mōv	mōv
metallurgy	**mĕ**·tə·lur·jee	me·**tăl**·ə·jee
methane	**mĕ**·thane	**mee**·thane
migraine	**mī**·grane	**mee**·grane
miniature	**min**·ē·ə·choor	**min**·ə·chə
missile	**mis**·əl	**mis**·īle
mobile	**mo**·bel	**mo**·bīle
mocha	**moh**·kə	**mŏ**·kə

WORD	US PRONUNCIATION	UK PRONUNCIATION
multi	**mul**·tī/**mul**·tee	**mul**·tee
myopic	mī·**ōp**·ic	mī·**ŏp**·ic
niche	nich	neesh
omega	ō·**may**·gə	ō·mə·gə
ordinarily	or·di·**nar**·i·lee	or·di·ner·i·lee
paparazzi	pa·pa·**rah**·tsi	pa·pa·**răt**·see
papier maché	**pāp**·er ma·**shay**	**păp**·ēay **mash**·ay
patent	**pă**·tent	**pā**·tent
pecan	pə·**cahn**	**pē**·căn
perfume	per·**fume**	**per**·fume
pipette	pīp·**et**	pĭ·**pĕt**
poinsettia	poin·**se**·tə	poin·**se**·tēə +
premature	**prē**·mə·**t(y)oor**	**prĕ**·mə·tyoor
premier	prə·**meer**/pree·**meer**	**prĕm**·ē·air
primarily	prī·**mar**·i·lee	prī·mĕr·ə·lee
privacy	**prī**·va·see	**prĭ**·va·see
process	**prŏ**·ses	**prō**·ses
produce	**prō**·doos	**prŏ**·dyoos
progress	**prŏ**·gres	**prō**·gres
protester	**prō**·tes·ter	prŏ·**test**·er
puma	**poo**·mə	**pyoo**·mə
quinine	**kwī**·nīn	**kwĭ**·neen
regatta	re·**gah**·tə	re·**gă**·tə
renaissance	**ren**·ə·sens	re·**nay**·sens
reveille	**rĕv**·a·lee	rə·**văl**·ee
route	rout/root	root
sahara	sə·**hă**·rə	sə·**hah**·rə

WORD	US PRONUNCIATION	UK PRONUNCIATION
salivary	**sal**·i·va·ree	sa·**lī**·va·ree
salve	săv	sălv
samba	**sahm**·ba	**săm**·ba
saucepan	**saus**·păn	**saus**·pən
schedule	**sked**·ule	**shed**·ule
semi	**se**·mī	**se**·mee +
shallot	**shăl**·ot	shə·**lot**
shone	shōn	shŏn
simultaneous	sī·mel·**tān**·ē·us	sĭ·mel·**tān**·ē·us
sloth	slōth	slōth
snooker	**snûk**·er	**snook**·er
solder	**sŏdd**·er	**sōld**·er
St. (in names such as *St. Albans*)	saint	sənt
status	**stă**·tus	**stā**·tus
strychnine	**strik**·nīn	**strik**·neen
tarpaulin	**tar**·pə·lin/tar·**pau**·lin	tar·**pau**·lin
temporarily	temp·or·**ar**·i·lee	**temp**·or·i·lee
thorough	**thû**·rō, **thu**·rō	**thu**·ra
tourniquet	**tour**·ni·ket	**tour**·ni·kay
trauma	**trah**·ma	**trau**·ma
trespass	**tres**·păs	**tres**·pəs
vase	vās (vahz if over $50)	vahz
vicarious	vī·**cair**·ē·us	vĭ·**cair**·ē·us
vitamin	**vī**·ta·min	**vĭ**·ta·min
vivacious	vī·**vā**·shas	vĭ·**vā**·shas
wigwam	**wig**·wahm	**wig**·wăm

WORD	US PRONUNCIATION	UK PRONUNCIATION
wont (custom)	wŏnt	wōnt
wrath	răth	rŏth
yogurt	**yō**·gert	**yŏ**·gert
z	zee	zed
zenith	**zē**·nith	**zĕn**·ith

SOME PERSONAL NAMES WITH DIFFERENT PRONUNCIATIONS

Here are a few names that are pronounced differently in the UK and the US. Sometimes Americans use the British pronunciations of personal names, however, when they are making reference to a specific person of British or Irish origin, such as George Bernard Shaw.

Pronunciation of Personal Names

WORD	US PRONUNCIATION	UK PRONUNCIATION
Bernard	ber·**nard**	**ber**·nəd
Cecil	**cē**·cil	**cĕ**·cil
Marie	mə·**ree**	**mah**·ree/**mă**·ree
Maurice	mau·**rees**	**morr**·is
Michel	mĭ·**shel**	**mee**·shel
Notre Dame	**nō**·ter dame	**nŏ**·tra·dahm +
Raleigh	**raw**·lee	**rah**·lee +
Renee	rə·**nay**	**rĕ**·nay
St. Augustine	saint **aug**·us·teen	sənt au·**gus**·tin
Van Gogh	van goh	van gof

For a guide to pronunciation symbols and other signs, see page vi.

⊰ 9 ⊱

Spelling

The lexicographer Noah Webster is responsible for many of the differences that distinguish American spelling from British spelling. His *American Dictionary of the English Language,* which came out in 1828, became the standard for US spelling. He originally wanted Americans to use much more strictly phonetic spelling, but he later compromised with only minor modifications. British spelling has also undergone reform since 1828. Most notably, *terror* and *horror* have lost their *–our* endings. The *–ise* suffix is relatively new to British spelling (see below).

The American spellings below are those preferred by *The American Heritage Dictionary of the English Language,* while the British spellings are those recommended by the *Shorter Oxford English Dictionary,* except in the case of words ending in *–ise* (see below). There are alternative ways of spelling some words.

Spelling Differences

US	UK
abridgment	abridgement
accouterment	accoutrement
acknowledgment	acknowledgement

For a guide to pronunciation symbols and other signs, see page vi.

US	UK
adapter +	adaptor
aging	ageing
aluminum	aluminium
ameba	amoeba +
analyze	analyse
anesthetic	anaesthetic
apologize +	apologise
appall	appal
appetizer +	appetiser
arbor	arbour
ardor	ardour
armor	armour
armorer	armourer
armory	armoury
artifact	artefact
authorize +	authorise
behavior	behaviour
behoove	behove
caliper	calliper
calisthenics	callisthenics
canceled	cancelled +
candor	candour
capitalize +	capitalise
catalog	catalogue
center	centre
chamomile	camomile
check (bank)	cheque
checkerboard	chequer-board

US	UK
chili	chilli
civilization +	civilisation
civilize +	civilise
clamor	clamour
clangor	clangour
clarinetist	clarinettist
color	colour
counselor	counsellor
cozy	cosy
curb (on a street)	kerb
czar	tsar
defense	defence
demeanor	demeanour
dependent *(noun)*	dependant
dialing	dialling
diarrhea	diarrhoea
disk	disc
distill	distil
dolor	dolour
draft	draught
economize +	economise
enamor	enamour
endeavor	endeavour
enroll	enrol
enthrall	enthral
equalize +	equalise
favor	favour
favorite	favourite

US	UK
favoritism	favouritism
fervor	fervour
fiber	fibre
flavor	flavour
fulfill	fulfil
furor	furore
gage	gauge +
gemology	gemmology
gray	grey +
harbor	harbour
harmonize +	harmonise
honor	honour
honorable	honourable
humor	humour
initialize +	initialise
inquiry +	enquiry
installment	instalment
instill	instil
jail	jail/gaol
jeweler	jeweller
jewelry	jewellery
judgment	judgement
labor	labour
license	licence
liter	litre
maneuver	manoeuvre
marvelous	marvellous
memorize +	memorise

US	UK
misdemeanor	misdemeanour
mobilize +	mobilise
mold	mould
molding	moulding
mom	mum
mustache	moustache
naught	nought
neighbor	neighbour
neighborhood	neighbourhood
normalize +	normalise
odor	odour
organize +	organise
pajamas	pyjamas
paralyze	paralyse
parlor	parlour
pasteurize +	pasteurise
peddler +	pedlar
percent	per cent
persnickety	pernickety
plow	plough
polarize +	polarise +
practice (verb)	practise
pretense	pretence
program	programme
pulverize +	pulverise
rancor	rancour
realize +	realise

US	UK
recognize +	recognise
rigor	rigour
rumor	rumour
savor	savour
savory	savoury
skeptic	sceptic
skillful	skilful
specter	spectre
spilled	spilt
splendor	splendour
story (of a building)	storey
succor	succour
sulfur	sulphur
symbolize +	symbolise
sympathize +	sympathise
theater	theatre +
tire	tyre
traveler	traveller
tumor	tumour
utilize +	utilise
valor	valour
vapor	vapour
vaporize +	vaporise
vigor	vigour
vise (tool)	vice
willful	wilful
worshiper	worshipper

When adding a suffix to a word ending with an *l* in the US, remember to double the last *l* only if the stress is on the second syllable of the root word, e.g., **trav·el**, *traveler* but *pat·rol*, *patrolling*. In Britain one always doubles the *l* in these words, e.g., *snorkel, snorkelling*.

Most words ending in *–our* in British spelling end in *or* in American spelling. Words ending with *–re* in British spelling usually end with *–er* in American spelling. *Theatre* is often spelled the British way.

The suffix *–ize* is still preferred by some British dictionaries for the following common words: *apologize, capitalize, equalize, finalize, legalize, mobilize, organize, pasteurize, popularize, realize, standardize, symbolize,* and *vaporize.* However, most Britons prefer the alternate *–ise* suffix with these words, which reflects the French influence on British English in the last 200 years. Some other common words that Americans spell with *z,* but Britons with *s,* include *analyze, cozy,* and *paralyze,* which are spelled *analyse, cosy,* and *paralyse* in British English.

Most words that have an *a* directly followed by an *e* in British English, such as *orthopaedics* and *anaesthesia,* are spelled without the *a* in American English. Similarly, the *o* is omitted in words such as *oedema, oestrogen, foetus,* and *oesophagus* in American English.

ONE-LETTER DIFFERENCES

Some words of special interest are those whose American and British spellings differ by just one letter, which, however, makes a difference in pronunciation. For the explanation of the origin of the difference between American *aluminum* and British *aluminium,* see page 76.

One-Letter Spelling Differences

US	UK
aluminum [a·**loo**·mi·num]	aluminium [al·yoo·**min**·ee·um]
carburetor [**kar**·bur·ay·ter]	carburettor [kar·bu·**re**·ta]
costumer	costumier [cos·**tyoo**·meeə]
crotch	crutch (crotch is also used)
divorcé/divorcée [di·**vor**·say]	divorcee [di·**vors**·ee]
doodad	doodah
greenskeeper	greenkeeper
hot flashes	hot flushes
jimmy	jemmy
mom	mum
muss up	mess up +
noodle (meaning "the head")	noddle
persnickety	pernickety
pita [**pē**·tə] (bread)	pitta [**pĭ**·ta]
plunk (down)	plonk
pudgy	podgy
putter	potter
salesroom	saleroom
sappy	soppy
specialty [**spesh**·al·tee]	speciality [spe·shee·**al**·i·tee]
tidbit	titbit

For a guide to pronunciation symbols and other signs, see page vi.

SOME DIFFERENCES IN PREPOSITIONAL USAGE

The preposition *of* is used more readily in the US following the word *all*, e.g., *all of my life, ouside of the US*. The use of the preposition *up* is not very common with the verb *to phone*. Most Americans would just say *I phoned him*. However, Americans do not use *ring* as a verb meaning "to call on the telephone," as in such phrases as *I will ring him tomorrow*, although they might say *I will give him a ring*. Sometimes Americans may say *pass up* instead of *pass* (e.g., *We passed them up a mile back*). Sometimes you may hear *change out* instead of *change* (e.g., *We had to change out the oil pump last year*), but this is not the preferred usage. Here are some other differences in prepositional usage.

Differences in the Use of Prepositions

US	UK
clue in	clue up
cut off (in traffic)	cut up
do over (make over)	do up
hold for ransom	hold to ransom
hold up/wait up	hold on +
in heat	on heat
in tow	on tow
sell out (property)	sell up
top off	top up
wait on (await)	wait for +
wait on (tables)	wait at

A plus sign [+] after a term indicates that the term is known in both the United Kingdom and the United States.

SOME DIFFERENCES IN THE USE OF SUFFIXES

British English and American English sometimes differ in the use of the suffixes *–ing* and *–ed*. In order to sound truly like a native, you should note the following differences.

Differences in the Use of Suffixes

US	UK
dance class	dancing class
dial tone	dialling tone
drainboard	draining board
driver's license	driving licence
file cabinet	filing cabinet +
fry pan	frying pan +
headed for	heading for +
race car	racing car
race meet	race meeting
rowboat	rowing boat
sailboat	sailing boat
sawed-off	sawn-off
scrub brush	scrubbing brush
swinging door	swing door

A plus sign [+] after a term indicates that the term is known in both the United Kingdom and the United States.

SOME DIFFERENT TERMS FOR PUNCTUATION

The British and American names for punctuation marks and other writing symbols also differ. The decimal point in the US is the same as a full stop, unlike the British decimal point, which is usually positioned halfway up the line, as in £1·50.

Punctuation Terms

US TERM	UK EQUIVALENT
[ ] brackets +	square brackets
{ } curly brackets	braces
( ) parentheses	brackets
/ slash +	stroke, oblique
✓ check mark	tick
! exclamation point	exclamation mark +
. period	full stop
" " quotation marks +	inverted commas

A plus sign [+] after a term indicates that the term is known in both the United Kingdom and the United States.

⇥ 10 ⇤

Sundry Terms

SOME DIFFERENT FURNISHING TERMS

Terms for different kinds of fabric and home furnishings may pose problems to Britons in America or to Americans in Britain. The following list should help sort the different words out.

Furnishing Terms

US	UK
area rug	rug (large)
baby carrier	carrycot
baseboard	skirting board
bassinet	crib
breakfront	display cabinet
buffet	sideboard
bureau	chest of drawers
cot	camp bed
couch +	settee +

For a guide to pronunciation symbols and other signs, see page vi.

US	UK
credenza [cra·**den**·za]	sideboard/cabinet for papers or supplies in an office
crib	cot
davenport	sofa +
drapes/draperies*	curtains
dresser	chest of drawers (often with a mirror)
dust ruffle	valance
floor lamp	standard lamp
hassock	pouffe
highboy	tallboy
hutch	dresser
lowboy	small dressing table
Murphy bed	foldaway bed
ottoman	footstool
pass-through	hatch
secretary desk	bureau/davenport
sheer curtains/sheers	net curtains
side server	sideboard +
trundle bed	truckle-bed
valance	pelmet

SOME DIFFERENT TERMS FOR TOOLS

Britons in the US or Americans in the UK who are lucky enough to extend their stay long enough to purchase a house or car may find this list useful.

Tools

US	UK
alligator clip	crocodile clip
blowtorch +	blowlamp
bone wrench	box spanner
boot (wheel immobilizer)	wheel clamp
coping saw	fretsaw
monkey wrench	pipe wrench +
utility knife	Stanley knife (a brand name)
Vise grips (brand name)	mole grips
wall anchor	Rawlplug (a brand name)
wrench +	spanner

A *plus sign* [+] after a term indicates that the term is known in both the United Kingdom and the United States.

SOME DIFFERENT MEDICAL TERMS

It is always unfortunate when we fall ill—or as Americans often say, *get sick*—but when it happens while we are staying in a foreign country, it can be particularly distressing when you don't know correct terms used to describe medical conditions and remedies. As a help to you in the doctor's office and elsewhere, here are some medical terms that differ between the US and the UK.

Medical Terms

US	UK
acetaminophen/Tylenol (brand)	paracetamol
anesthesiologist	anaesthetist
appendectomy +	appendicectomy
Baker-acted *(regional slang)*	sectioned

A *plus sign* [+] after a term indicates that the term is known in both the United Kingdom and the United States.

US	UK
charge nurse	ward sister (female)/charge nurse (male)
chronic fatigue syndrome +	ME (myalgic encephalomyelitis)
circulating nurse	theatre sister
crib death	cot-death
diaper	nappy
doctor's office	doctor's surgery
EKG	ECG +
emergency department +	A and E/Accident and Emergency
gurney	stretcher +
IV	drip
in isolation	in a barrier/isolation ward
intern	houseman
internist	specialist in internal diseases
lidocaine	lignocaine
locum tenens (rarely used by a layperson in the US)	locum
infectious mononucleosis +	glandular fever
operating room	operating theatre/theatre
pacifier	dummy
physical therapist	physiotherapist
PMS (premenstrual syndrome) +	PMT (premenstrual tension)
podiatrist	chiropodist (similar)
Q-Tip (brand name)	cotton swab +
prenatal +	antenatal
resident doctor	registrar
RN +	sister
scrubs/scrub suit	theatre whites/theatre garb
shot (*colloq.*, injection) +	jab

US	UK
specialist	consultant (similar)
sponge bath	blanket bath
(a) surgery	operation +
tongue depressor	spatula
visiting nurse	district community nurse
walker	walking frame/Zimmer frame

Some medical terms are also spelled differently in the UK and the US. See page 90.

CARNIVAL (FUNFAIR) TERMS

One interesting area in which British and American usages differs is in the words used at carnivals, or as the British call them, funfairs.

Carnival Terms

UK	US
big wheel	Ferris wheel
candyfloss	cotton candy
Dodgem cars	bumper cars +
merry-go-round +	carousel
sideshow location	midway
steam organ	calliope [ka·lī·ō·pee]
switchback	roller coaster +
toffee apple	candy apple/caramel apple

A plus sign [+] after a term indicates that the term is known in both the United Kingdom and the United States.

SOME DIFFERENT GARDENING TERMS

Americans often think of Britons as people devoted to gardens and skilled at maintaining them. Here are a few gardening terms that differ between the two countries. (Many plant names are pronounced differently in the US and the UK as well. See pages 77–83.)

Gardening Terms

UK	US
busy Lizzie	impatiens
casuarina	Australian pine
dead-head	remove dead flower heads
Norfolk pine	Norfolk Island pine
rockery	rock garden +
secateurs	pruners/pruning shears
trug	shallow gardening basket
minimal-irrigation landscaping	Xeriscaping

A *plus sign* [+] after a term indicates that the term is known in both the United Kingdom and the United States.

⊰ 11 ⊱

What Not to Say

WORDS AND TERMS THAT A BRITON SHOULD AVOID IN THE US

Britons and Americans can usually understand each other very well with a little effort. Any casual misunderstandings that occur can usual be sorted out quite quickly. However, there are a few words and expressions that sometimes pose more serious problems. The following is a list of common British terms and phrases that can mean something quite different in the US.

What Not to Say in the US

Brilliant (slang)	Use *great* or *cool.*
Carry on	Use *go ahead* or *after you.*
Cheers	Use *thanks* or *goodbye* if used in a slang sense.
Dear	This is not used often in the US for *expensive.*
Estate agent	Could be misunderstood. Use *realtor.*
Fag	This is an offensive term meaning "gay man" in the US. Use *cigarette.*
Fagged out	This phrase will remind Americans of the words *fag* and *faggot.* Use *beat* or *whipped.*

Faggot	This is an offensive term meaning "gay man" in the US. There is no exact equivalent for the name of the traditional English dish called a *faggot*, so the British expression must be explained with a phrase such as *meatball made from pork liver, onions, and bread*.
Give me a tinkle	Could sound vulgar. Try *Give me a call* or *Give me a jingle* instead.
Homely	This means *unattractive* in the US. Try *homey*.
I knocked myself up (a quick meal)	I *prepared* or *put together* a meal.
Keep your pecker up	Vulgar in the US. Try *Keep smiling*.
Knock up	When playing tennis, use *warm up*.
Knock me up	A vulgar expression in the US. Try *Wake me up*.
Lay the table	Use instead *Set the table*.
May I top you up?	Would not be understood in the US. Try *Want me to top that off?* or *May I freshen your drink?*
My mate	A *mate* in the US usually refers to a marriage partner. Try *my buddy*.
No naked lights	Use *No open flames*.
Pot plant	This would mean a marijuana plant to most Americans. Try *house plant*.
Potty about	Would not be understood in the US. Try *crazy about*.
Ring me up	Use *Give me a call*.
Rubber	This is an informal word for a condom in the US. Use *eraser*.

Sleeping partner	Use *silent partner.*
Solicitor	Use *attorney* or *lawyer.*
Tramp	Use *hobo* or *homeless person.* *Tramp* can also mean "loose woman."
Wash up	In the US this expression means "to wash your face and/or hands." Use instead *wash the dishes.*
Where's the ladies'/gents'?	Use *Where's the ladies'/women's/men's room?* or *Where's the restroom?*

WORDS AND TERMS THAT AN AMERICAN SHOULD AVOID IN THE UK

The following is a list of common American terms and phrases that may confuse or offend Britons.

What Not to Say in the UK

Vest, suspenders, and *pants*	These refer to undergarments in the UK. Instead, use *waistcoat, braces,* and *trousers* respectively.
Knickers	This term means "panties" in the UK. Use *knickerbockers.*
Get the poop on	Use instead *Get the low-down on.*
I'm stuffed	Possibly vulgar. Use *I'm full.*
Bugger	An offensive word in British English.
Bummer	Use instead *nuisance* or *disappointing.*
Bum steer	Use instead *bad advice* or *bad directions.*
Fanny	Vulgar. Use *bottom* or *behind.*
Fanny pack	Possibly vulgar. Use *bumbag.*

Get a bang out of someone	Possibly vulgar. Use *get a kick out of someone.*
Tramp	Only use this if you mean "hobo." It is never used to refer to a loose woman in the UK.
School	This is not used for *university* or *higher education* in the UK.
Shagging flies	This might not only sound obscene, but impossible. Try *retrieving and returning baseballs.*
Wash up	This means "wash the dishes" in Britain. Try *wash your hands* instead.

SOME WORDS WITH DIFFERENT MEANINGS

The following words have quite different meanings in the United States and the United Kingdom.

Words with Different Meanings

WORD	US MEANING	UK MEANING
academician	an academic	member of an academy
basket case	exhausted person	insane person
billion	one thousand million	one million million
bomb (especially of a play)	go badly	go very well
bucket shop	disreputable high-pressure brokerage firm	travel agency specializing in discount tickets
bureau	chest of drawers	secretary desk
casket	coffin	small ornamental box

WORD	US MEANING	UK MEANING
cohort	colleage/supporter	group of people representing a common cause
cordial	liqueur	concentrated fruit juice
cot	makeshift bed	baby's bed
cranky	irritable	eccentric
crockery	earthenware pots	plates and dishes
creek	stream	narrow tidal inlet
cruet	small vinegar container	container for condiments
cutlery	knives	eating utensils
cut up	fool around	feel upset
davenport	sofa	writing desk
deadhead	drive without a load	dead flower
diddle	waste time	swindle
dormitory	building used for sleeping	room used for sleeping
dresser	chest of drawers	display cabinet for china
dry goods	fabrics and clothing	foodstuffs
fag	(*offensive slang*) gay man	cigarette
garden	cultivated area for plants	lawn and flower-beds
green card	permanent resident card	motorists' foreign insurance
hassock	round stuffed cushion on the floor	church kneeling cushion
homely	ugly	cozy/unpretentious
jug	tall vessel with a narrow neck and perhaps a stopper	any vessel with a pouring lip (called *pitcher* in the US)

WORD	US MEANING	UK MEANING
jumper	pinafore dress	sweater
knickers	knee-length trousers	panties
knock up	*(vulgar slang)* make pregnant	wake up
leery	wary	sly
loft	open, elevated area in a room	attic
luminary	candle used to light the way	leader in a subject
marquee	illuminated promotional sign	outdoor tent for parties
mean	nasty	stingy
momentarily	in a moment	for a moment
mutt	mongrel	dog *(slang)*
nervy	impudent	nervous
outhouse	outdoor toilet	shed near a house
pantomime	show performed by a mime artist	Christmas theatrical performance
pavement	road surface	paved pedestrian pathway
phonograph	record player	early musical player operating off cylinders
pissed	angry	drunk
proctor	exam supervisor at a university	disciplinary officer at a university
pumps	ladies' dress shoes	canvas sneakers
ratty	shabby	irritable
redcap	railway porter	military police officer
school	any learning institute	institute for teaching children

WORD	US MEANING	UK MEANING
shingle	asphalt roof tile/ small sign	wooden roof tile/ beach pebble
skivvies	underwear	maids (A *skivvy* is a maid.)
slate (verb)	put on an agenda	criticize
slot machine	gambling machine	vending machine
snifter	brandy glass	small alcoholic drink
snookered	conned	trapped
Social Security	government pension for retirees	Welfare
solitaire	card game for one person	board game with pegs
suspenders	trouser supports	stocking supports
table (verb)	put a bill aside temporarily	bring forward for discussion
tick off	annoy	reprimand
tuition	college fees	tutoring/teaching
twister	tornado	swindler
valance	covering over a curtain rod	skirt around a bed
vest	sleeveless garment worn under a jacket	undershirt
video	videotape	videotape/tape player
wash up	wash oneself	wash the dishes
yard	lawn around a house	paved area

⊰ 12 ⊱

Idioms and Expressions

SOME BRITISH EXPRESSIONS

Here is a list comparing British expressions with similar expressions used in the US. Sometimes there is no common equivalent. In this case, the equivalents given in italics are simply explanations of the expression and are not idioms.

British Expressions

UK	US
at the end of one's tether	at the end of one's rope
bang on	right on (the nose)
basket case	insane person
bat an eyelid	bat an eye
beat them hollow	clean their clocks
belt up!	shut up! +
blot one's copybook	*hurt one's reputation*
blow the gaff	spill the beans +
Bob's your uncle!	And there you have it!
bright spark	smart cookie

For a guide to pronunciation symbols and other signs, see page vi.

UK	US
browned off	teed off
bung it on	blow smoke
bunk off	play hookey
carry the can	hold the bag
channel-hop	channel-surf
chat up	come on to
cheesed off	teed off
chock-a-block full	chock-full
clapped out	*worn out*
clean one's teeth	brush one's teeth
clue up on	clue in on
come a cropper	*fall down*
common or garden	garden-variety
cot-case	basket case
(a) dab hand at something	a crackerjack at something
daylight robbery	highway robbery
(a) dead cert	You can take it to the bank.
different as chalk and cheese	*comparing two very different people*
do a moonlight flit	*sneak out in the night*
do the dirty on someone	give someone the shaft
down at heel	poor/unkempt
drive round the bend	drive up a wall +
drop a clanger	*make a big faux pas*
drunk as a lord	drunk as a skunk
dull as ditchwater	dull as dishwater
feel hard-done-by	*feel that you were treated unfairly*
feel peckish	have the munchies
fit someone up	frame someone

UK	US
from the year dot	from the year one
full marks for	deserves an A for
get off with someone	make out with someone
get the gen on	get the poop on
get the wind up	get all shook up *(colloq.)*
get your come-uppance	get your just deserts
get your knickers in a twist	have a hissy fit
give it a miss	skip it/pass it up +
give someone the pip	annoy someone
give someone their cards	give someone a pink slip
give someone their marching orders	give someone their walking papers
give someone the vees/ V sign	give someone the finger/bird (In the UK, both the index and the middle finger, spread in a V-shape, are used to make a vulgar gesture.)
go bust	go broke
go like the clappers	*go at great speed*
go spare	go berserk +
happy as a sandboy	happy as a clam
Hard cheese!	Tough!
have a lie-in	sleep in +
have a natter	shoot the breeze
have no truck with	*have no dealings with*
have your guts for garters	you'll be dead meat
heap of	bunch of
Heath Robinson device	Rube Goldberg device
hell for leather	hell-bent for leather
home and dry	home free

UK	US
if the cap fits	if the shoe fits
in a funk	*frightened*
in a trice	in a heartbeat/in a New York minute
in donkey's years	in forever
in future	in the future
in queer street	up the creek +
in someone's good books	in someone's good graces +
jump the lights	run a red light
keep your pecker up	keep your chin up +
knock-on effect	domino effect +
knock spots off	knock the socks off
knocked for six	thrown for a loop
land someone with	stick someone with
land up	end up +
left holding the baby	left holding the bag
left to carry the can	left holding the bag
long in the tooth	*old*
look at someone old-fashioned	give someone a disapproving look
look like death warmed up	look like death warmed over
lumber someone with	*encumber with*
make heavy weather of something	*make an ordeal out of something*
money for old rope	*easy money*
much of a muchness	*much the same*
mug up on	bone up on
Not on your nelly!	No way! +
not the done thing	not socially acceptable

UK	US
Now you're *for* it!	You're dead meat!
off one's trolley	off one's rocker +
off the beaten track	off the beaten path
on my tod	on my lonesome
on tenterhooks	on pins and needles
on the dole	on unemployment
on the never-never	in installments
on toast	over a barrel +
O.T.T.	over the top
out on the tiles	*out having a wild time*
over the moon	ecstatic
Pack it in!	Stop it!
packed up	went kaput
panic stations	*pandemonium*
past praying for	*beyond hope*
peg out (die)	check out
play gooseberry	chaperone someone
potter around	putter around
preaching to the converted	preaching to the choir
pull your socks up	try harder
put it on the slate	put it on the tab
put someone's nose out of joint	*upset someone*
Rolls Royce of	Cadillac of
rough diamond +	diamond in the rough
rub up the wrong way	rub the wrong way
run with the hare and hunt with the hounds	play both ends against the middle +

UK	US
sale or return	on consignment
save one's bacon	save one's skin
send someone to Coventry	give someone the silent treatment
sharp as a needle	sharp as a tack
skeleton in the cupboard	skeleton in the closet
slap-up (of a meal)	bang-up
slowcoach	slowpoke
small beer	small potatoes
snookered [**snoo**·kerd]	behind the eight ball
Sod it!	Screw it!
soldier on	press on +
spend a penny	use the bathroom/go potty
spot on	on the money/on the nose
stand for office	run for office
Stone the crows!	Holy cow!
stop on a sixpence	stop on a dime
storm in a teacup	a tempest in a teapot
sure as eggs are eggs	sure as shootin'
suss it out	scope it out
take a recce [**rek**·kee]	check it out +
take the biscuit	take the cake +
take the mickey out of someone	razz someone
talk nineteen to the dozen	talk up a blue streak
talk the hind legs off a donkey	talk up a storm
tart up +	gussy up
ten a penny	a dime a dozen

UK	US
the book of words	*the instruction book*
The game's up!	The jig is up!
The penny dropped.	The light came on.
the tricky bit	the tricky part
thin as a rake	skinny as a rail
third time lucky	three times a charm
throw a spanner in the works	throw a monkey wrench in the works
tick off (See *tick off* in the list of American expressions below.)	*reprimand*
tinker's cuss	tinker's damn
too big for his boots	too big for his britches
top off	*assassinate*
twopenny-halfpenny [tuppeny-haypenny]	two-bit (inferior)
up my street	up my alley
went like a bomb	*took off, was a hit*
when it comes to the crunch	when push comes to shove +
with knobs on	in spades
wouldn't touch it with a barge pole	wouldn't touch it with a ten-foot pole
yell blue murder	yell bloody murder
You're having me on!	You're putting me on!

SOME AMERICAN EXPRESSIONS

Here is a list comparing US expressions with similar expressions used in Britain. Sometimes there is no common equivalent. In this case, the equivalents given in italics are simply explanations

of the expression and are not idioms. Pronunciations are en-
closed in square brackets.

American Expressions

US	UK
(to be) a day late and a dollar short	*miss out on something*
a dime a dozen	ten a penny
all kinds of (colloquial meaning)	*a large number of*
all tied up (in sports)	tied +
any more you don't	these days you don't
at the end of one's rope	at the end of one's tether
bang-up	slap-up
barhopping	going on a pub crawl
basket case	cot-case
be all shook up	get the wind up
beat up on	beat up +
beat up on oneself	*berate oneself*
behind the eight ball	snookered/stuffed
bigtime	in a big way/and how!
blow off someone	*dismiss/ignore someone*
blow smoke	bung it on
bone up on	mug up on
bring someone up to speed	*bring someone up to date*
brush one's teeth	clean one's teeth
buffalo *(verb)*	*to confuse for gain*
bug out	scarper/sneak out
(a) bum rap	a raw deal +
(a) bum steer	*bad advice/bad directions*

For a guide to pronunciation symbols and other signs, see page vi.

US	UK
bummed me out	*upset me* +
burned me up	browned me off
Butt out!	Stop butting in!
Cadillac of	Rolls Royce of
call the law (regional South)	*call the police*
can't get blood out of a turnip	can't get blood out of a stone +
catch some rays	get some sun
catch some z's [zeez]	have a zizz
catty-corner from	*diagonally across from*
catty-wumpus	crooked
check out (to die)	peg out
Chill out! *(slang)*	Calm down! +
chock-full	chock-a-block full
clean their clocks	beat them hollow
close the barn door after the horse is out	close the stable door after the horse has bolted
close, but no cigar	nearly made it! +
clue in on	clue up on
come on to	chat up
come unglued	*go crazy*
compare apples and oranges	*compare two different things*
compare apples with apples	*compare things in a similar category*
cool one's jets	*dampen one's ardour*
cotton-pickin' hands	filthy hands
cotton to someone	*take a liking to someone*
cotton up to	suck up to +
crack a window	*open a window a crack*

US	UK
crackerjack at something *(noun)*	a dab hand at something
crazy as a loon	have bats in the belfry/batty
cry uncle	*admit defeat*
cut loose	*go wild*
cut up	act the fool/muck about
(a) diamond in the rough	a rough diamond
do a double take	*take a closer look at something surprising that had gone unnoticed*
do a number on	hurt/damage
do a snow job	*attempt to deceive or persuade through flattery or exaggeration*
doesn't know beans about it	knows bugger all about it
dog and pony show	*farcical happening*
doggone	ruddy
don't give a hill of beans	don't care either way
Don't go there!	*Keep off that topic!*
Don't take any wooden nickels!	Don't be conned!
down the pike	down the line +
down to the wire	*running out of time*
duke it out	*fight it out*
dull as dishwater	dull as ditchwater
every which way	*in all directions*
exact same	very same
feel punk	*feel unwell*
fill out a form +	fill in a form
first dibs on	first option on
first off	*firstly*
fit to be tied	*beside oneself with rage*

US	UK
flip someone the bird *(slang)*	give someone the vees
fresh out of	*just ran out of*
from soup to nuts	*all-inclusive*
from the get-go	from the word go +
from the year one	from the year dot
garden-variety	common or garden
get a charge/bang out of	get a kick out of +
get the best of	get the better of +
get the skinny on	get the lowdown on +
gets old	gets tedious/dull +
Give me some sugar!	Give me a kiss!
give someone a licking	give someone a hiding
give someone a pink slip	give someone their cards
give someone the bum's rush	abruptly dismiss someone
give someone the finger +	make a V sign
give someone the shaft	do the dirty on someone
give someone the silent treatment	send someone to Coventry
give someone his/her walking papers	give someone his/her marching orders
go ballistic	go berserk
go belly up	go under +
go broke	go bust
go Dutch treat	go Dutch
Go figure!	*Try and figure that one out!*
go potty	spend a penny
good to go	all set
goof off *(verb)*	skive off
grandfathered in	*permitted because of preexisting conditions*

US	UK
graveyard shift	night shift
grossed me out *(hip slang)*	*disgusted me*
gussy up	tart up
hang a right/hang a left	*turn right/turn left*
happy as a clam	happy as a sandboy
haul ass *(vulgar)*	*move along*
have a hissy fit	get your knickers in a twist
have a tin ear	be tone-deaf +
Have at it!	Go to it!
have the munchies	feel peckish
held for ransom	*held to ransom*
hell-bent for leather	hell for leather
hem and haw	hum and ha
hightail it	*go at top speed*
highway robbery	daylight robbery
hit the sack	hit the hay +
hogtied	*restrained/thwarted*
Holy cow!	Stone the crows!
home free	home and dry
I wouldn't bet the ranch on it.	I wouldn't stake my life on it.
I'll have your job.	*I'll get you fired.*
if the shoe fits	if the cap fits
in a (blue) funk	*feeling depressed*
in a heartbeat/in a New York minute	in a trice/in two ticks
in back	in the back +
in back of	behind +
in forever	in donkey's years

US	UK
in hock	*pawned*
in the loop *(hip)*	*in the know*
just shy of	*almost/coming up on*
kick butt *(hip slang)*	*stir people up*
kitty-corner from	*diagonally across from*
Knock yourself out!	Go for it!
left holding the bag	left holding the baby
let go	made redundant
lie like a rug *(verb)*	lie through one's teeth +
like gangbusters	*with a lot of energy*
like it's going out of style	*selling fast*
look like a train wreck	*look disheveled*
look like death warmed over	look like death warmed up
low-rent	low-class
luck out	*be very lucky*/be in luck +
make out (with someone)	get off (with someone)
make out like a bandit	*to get a bargain/be very successful*
make over *(noun)*	face-lift +
make over *(verb)*	do up
more bang for your buck	*more for your money*
nip and tuck	touch and go +
Now we're cooking with gas.	*Now we're on track.*
off the beaten path	off the beaten track
off the rack (clothing)	off the peg
on consignment	sale or return
on my lonesome	on my tod
on pins and needles	on tenterhooks

US	UK
on the fritz	on the blink +
on the lam	on the run +
on the money	spot-on
on the nose	spot-on
on the wrong side of the tracks	*in the wrong part of town*
out of pocket (Southern)	*can't be reached*
out of town	away
paint oneself into a corner	drive into a corner
party animal	raver, someone who acts rowdily at parties
party pooper	*someone who spoils a party*
perk up one's ears	prick up one's ears +
Philadelphia lawyer	*genius*
pick up a room	*tidy a room*
pig out	*make a pig of oneself*
play both ends against the middle +	run with the hare and hunt with the hounds
play hookey	bunk off
play phone tag	*to call each other's answering machine without speaking in person*
pooped	knackered
press the flesh	*shake hands with supporters*
put in one's two cents	*give unsolicited advice*
put it on the tab +	put it on the slate
put out *(vulgar slang)*	make oneself sexually available to someone, be sexually active
put the moves on	chat up

US	UK
putter around	potter around
rack up	clock up/notch up
railroad someone (convict hastily and unjustly)	press-gang someone
rattled my cage	wound me up
razz someone	take the mickey out of someone
ride shotgun *(verb)*	to ride in the passenger seat
right on	spot on/bang on
rub elbows with	rub shoulders with +
rub the wrong way	rub up the wrong way
Rube Goldberg device	Heath Robinson device
run a red light	jump the lights
run for office	stand for office
Run that by me again?	*Would you repeat that?*
same difference	same thing +
scarf down	scoff down
scope it out	take a recce/suss it out
set up housekeeping	set up home
sharp as a tack	sharp as a needle
shine up to	suck up to +
shoo-in *(noun)*	dead cert (certainty)
shoot from the hip	tell it the way it is
shoot hoops	*play basketball*
shoot the breeze/bull	have a natter
Shoot!	Bother (it)!
skeleton in the closet	skeleton in the cupboard
skinny as a rail	thin as a rake
skip it/pass it up +	give it a miss

US	UK
sleep over *(verb)* (children's term)	*spend the night*
slip someone a Mickey	slip someone a Mickey Finn
slowpoke	slowcoach
small potatoes	small beer
smart cookie	bright spark
snookered [**snû**·kerd]	conned + (see *snookered* UK)
Son of a gun!	Well, I never!
Sounds like Greek to me. +	It's all double Dutch to me.
stand on/in line	stand in a queue
step up to the plate	come forward and make a stand
stick someone with	lumber/land someone with
stop on a dime	stop on a sixpence
sure as shootin'	sure as eggs
take the cake +	take the biscuit
talk up a storm	talk the hind legs off a donkey
teed off	browned off/cheesed off
tempest in a teapot	a storm in a teacup
The light came on.	The penny dropped.
the whole ball of wax	the whole (kit and) caboodle +
the whole nine yards	the whole (kit and) caboodle +
three times a charm	third time lucky
throw a monkey wrench in the works	throw a spanner in the works
throw someone a curved ball	bowl a googly
thrown for a loop	knocked sideways/knocked for six
tick off (See *tick off* in Some British Expressions, page 114.)	cheese off/*annoy*
to go (at a fast-food restaurant)	to take away

US	UK
too big for his britches	too big for his boots
toss one's cookies	*vomit*
Tough!	Hard cheese!
two-bit (inferior)	twopenny-halfpenny (pronounced [tuppeny-haypenny])
up and at' em	up and at it
up my alley	up my street
up the creek +	in queer street
wait on line	stand in a queue
want out	want to get out
water over the dam	water under the bridge +
Way to go!	Good going!
way too	much too
We're history. *(slang)*	Let's get going.
went kaput	packed up
What a bummer!	*What a nuisance!*
What a stitch!	What a hoot! +
When pigs fly!	Pigs might fly!
when push comes to shove +	when it comes to the crunch
whipped	knackered
wouldn't touch it with a ten-foot pole	wouldn't touch it with a barge pole
yea high	so high +
yell bloody murder	yell blue murder
You can take it to the bank.	It's a dead cert.
You'll be dead meat.	They'll have your guts for garters.
You're dead meat!	Now you're *for* it!
You're putting me on!	You're having me on!

To *put one's best foot forward* means "to do one's best" in the US. In Britain it also means to walk briskly. To *cotton to* someone means to take a liking to someone in the US. In British English to *cotton on* means to catch on to an idea. To be *at loose ends* in the US means to be in a dither. If you are *at a loose end* in Britain it means that you have nothing much to do. To *feel one's oats* means to feel lively in British English, but in American English it means to feel self-important. If you are *snookered* in Britain, you are unable to get out of a difficult situation. If you have been *snookered* in the US, you have been conned. *Tick off* in the US means "annoy," but it has a totally different meaning in the UK, where it means "reprimand."

COMMON METAPHORICAL BASEBALL TERMS

Americans often use sports terms in conversations. One sport from which a lot of terms are borrowed is baseball, which, by the way, evolved from the British game called *rounders*.

Baseball Expressions

US	UK
a ballpark figure	a rough estimate
a tough call	a difficult decision
The bases are loaded.	It's a make-or-break situation.
batting a thousand	going great guns
batting zero	getting nowhere
cover all bases	take care of everything
didn't get to first base	didn't accomplish anything
get to home base	achieve one's goal
go to bat for someone	be someone's advocate
off-base, to be	to hold a mistaken idea

UK	US
out in left field	off track
screwball (a ball pitched with reverse spin)	eccentric or irrational person
step up to the plate	make a stand
strike out	fail
switch hitter	bisexual person
throw someone a curve (ball)	throw someone a googly
touch base	get in touch with someone
whole new ball game	completely different situation
You're up./You're at bat.	It's up to you./It's your turn.

In the US, playing *pepper* means warming up by catching and returning balls. Practicing catching balls in the outfield is known as *shagging flies.*

SOME OLDER BRITISH WORDS AND EXPRESSIONS

The following old-fashioned words are sometimes encountered in older books and films, and you can sometimes even hear them being used by some people in speech, occasionally in jest.

Older British Expressions

UK	US
Bath chair	wheelchair
bathing drawers	bathing suit
beaker	mug
bottom gear	first gear
bounder	scoundrel
carriage rug	lap robe
char/charwoman	cleaning lady

UK	US
Cheese it!	Stop it!
charabanc	tour bus
cloth-eared	hard of hearing
counterpane	bedspread
(a) gas	a laugh
geyser	instant hot water heater
hangover (a relic)	holdover
identification parade	lineup (police)
ironmonger	hardware store
keypuncher	card punch operator
old lag	habitual convict
outside (on a bus)	upstairs
push-bike	bike
ripping	terrific
rum	odd/strange
shape	Jell-O (brand name)
shooting brake	station wagon
wireless	radio
wood-wool	excelsior

SOME OLDER AMERICAN WORDS AND EXPRESSIONS

Older Americans may continue using regional pronunciations of words such as [**may**·zhure] and [**play**·zhure] for *measure* and *pleasure*. *Rations* may be pronounced [**ray**·shns], and *long-lived* may sometimes be pronounced [long-līved] with a long vowel as in *alive*. This is actually the "correct" pronunciation from a historical point of view, since the word was formed from the noun *life* in Middle English using the same pattern as *hook-nosed* or *ruddy-faced*. The common modern pronunciation with a short vowel is a more recent development based on an association of the phrase *long-lived* with forms of the verb *to live*.

Here is a list of some old-fashioned expressions that may be encountered in novels and films and under other such circumstances, and some older people may occasionally be heard to use these expressions. Younger people may even use some of them from time to time in jest.

Older American Expressions

US	UK
aforenoon	morning
apple polisher	one who curries favour with another
barnburner	an exciting event
blues harp	mouth-organ
bodacious	remarkable/outstanding
broad/gal/dame	chick/bird
bumbershoot	brolly
C-note/C	one-hundred-dollar bill
card punch operator	keypuncher/keypunch operator
cheaters	reading glasses
chew the fat/chew the rag	have a natter
church key	a beverage can or bottle opener
colored glasses	sunglasses
comfort station	public convenience
copacetic	A-OK +
cowpoke	cowboy
(to) cut a rug	to dance
dimestore/five-and-ten	low-cost general store

US	UK
dime-store glasses	reading glasses purchased without a prescription
directional	indicator
dressing (with poultry)	stuffing
druggist	pharmacist
excelsior (former brand name)	wood-wool
fireplug	fire hydrant
five-spot/fin	a five-dollar bill
fly window (of a car)	quarter-light
For land's sake!	Oh, my giddy aunt!
gandy dancer	platelayer (railway)
gobs of	bags of
goose egg (a score of zero)	duck/duck's egg
have one's druthers	have one's way
high-test (gas)	high-octane
hoofer	professional dancer
icebox	refrigerator
in a coon's age	in donkey's years
in the back forty (humorous)	at the bottom of the garden
lap robe	rug (light blanket)
lickety-split	hell for leather
light bill	electricity bill
milquetoast	wimp
monkeyshines	monkey tricks
normal school	teacher training college
oleo	margarine
phonograph	gramophone
phosphate	soft drink

US	UK
pill	a disagreeable person
pocketbook	purse/handbag
puff	eiderdown
put on the dog	put on side
quinine water	Indian tonic water
ride herd	supervise/boss
ride Shank's mare	take Shanks's pony
sawbuck	ten-dollar bill
sawing logs	sleeping
seltzer bottle	soda siphon
shag	dance
sock hop	1950s-style dance
soda jerk	someone who works at a soda fountain
spider (regional North and Atlantic)	frying pan
steamer rug	rug
strike pay dirt	on the scent
swell	dandy
trade-last/TL	a compliment that one person passes on to another in exchange for a compliment about himself or herself
two bits	twenty-five cents (25¢)
Victrola (brand name)	wind-up gramophone
visiting fireman	special visitor in town
warm over (food)	warm up
What the Sam Hill?	What the hell?
white gas	unleaded petrol
wing window (car)	quarter-light
wood alcohol	methyl alcohol

⊰ 13 ⊱

Notes on Symbols and Abbreviations

THE ℞ SYMBOL

The symbol ℞ (often written as R with a small x to the side) is seen a lot in the US. It was originally an abbreviation for the Latin word *recipe,* the command form of the verb *recipere* "to take," used by doctors when writing prescriptions. A large ℞ symbol is sometimes displayed on the street sign identifying a business as a pharmacy. In general, the symbol serves to convey the idea of a prescription or remedy. It is often used in everyday print, e.g., *Do you have heartburn? ℞: a short walk after meals.*

THE $ SYMBOL

One often hears that the dollar symbol ($) was created by super-imposing the letter *U* over the letter *S* with the bottom of the *U* cut off. An interesting idea, but it has no validity. Several other theories have been proposed.

During the 1700s, a Spanish coin (the *peso*) popularly called a dollar was the most widely used form of currency both in the original 13 colonies governed by Britain and also in the newly independent United States. The word *dollar* at that time was used for various coins that were modeled on a Bohemian coin called the *Joachimsthaler*, named after the silver mine at Joachimstal (now Jáchymov). This town, which is now in the Czech Republic, first minted coins in 1519. The Spanish dollar had various other names, such as *the pillar dollar* or *a piece of eight*. The name *pillar dollar* came from the image engraved on the front of the coin, which represented two pillars, the Pillars of Hercules at Gibraltar, draped in a banner. This image may have developed into the dollar sign, the pillars somehow becoming the vertical lines. Other theories about the origin of the symbol $ have been advocated, however. For instance, it may have developed from the letter *P*, an abbreviation for Spanish *peso,* plus a small *s* written beside it to indicate the plural.

The Spanish coin was frequently cut like a pie into eight wedge-shaped pieces, hence the name *piece of eight*. Until recently, this way of making change was reflected in the practice of using quarters and eighths of a dollar in trading on the American stock market. However, American stock markets switched to a decimal system using cents in April 2002. An old slang term for the 25-cent coin is *two bits*—of a *piece of eight,* that is—and the coin is still almost always called a *quarter* in everyday speech. The first US dollar was minted in 1794 and is known as the *flowing hair dollar* from the image of a man with long flowing hair featured on the coin.

THE £ SYMBOL

The pound, also called the *pound sterling,* is represented by the symbol £. It is an elaboration of an *L* standing for Latin *libra* meaning a pound (the unit of weight). Historically, the terms *pound* and *pound sterling* originated in medieval times, when a coin called a *sterling* was the basic monetary unit. The sum of 240 sterlings, which weighed a pound, was known as a *pound of sterling,* and later a *pound*. The pound was initially convertible into silver and later into gold. The gold standard was abandoned in 1931.

THE # SYMBOL

In the US the symbol # before a number means "number," rather like "no.," which is used in both countries. If placed after a number, it means pounds (weight). For example, #3 means "number 3," whereas 3# means "three pounds." This symbol is usually called the *pound sign* in the US. Many years ago it was known as the *tick-tack-toe sign* or the *number sign*. The pound sign is rarely used in Britain, and the British terms for the symbol #, *hash*, *gate*, and *square*, are unknown in the US. The American term *pound sign* can cause confusion, since this term can refer either to the symbol # or to the symbol £.

PLC/LTD

The abbreviation *plc* stands for *Public Limited Company* and is often seen at the end of a company's name in the UK. The abbreviation *Ltd* is also used. These abbreviations have a similar meaning to the abbreviation *Inc.*, often seen at the end of an American company's name. There is usually a comma preceding the letters *Inc.*, but not preceding *plc* or *Ltd*.

⫷ 14 ⫸

Miscellaneous Information

I have noticed several other differences between British English and American English that either do not fit into any particular category or are more of general interest than any practical use.

- Americans will often say "two times" rather than "twice," as in "We saw the show two times."

- When spelling a word aloud that has two consecutive identical letters, most Britons will use the word *double*. For example, to spell *canned*, Britons will say *"c-a-double n-e-d."* Most Americans, however, will pronounce each letter separately: *"c-a-n-n-e-d."*

- The date on a form or a letter in Britain is expressed by putting the day, the month, then the year (10 December, 2004). In the US the month comes first, followed by the day and then the year (December 10, 2004).

- Hours and minutes are divided by a period in Britain, but by a colon in the US (9:30 a.m. in the US, 9.30 a.m. in the UK).

- *To feel sick* in British English means to feel nauseated. To express this feeling an American would say he *felt sick to his stomach.*

- The term *tarmac* is used in the US only when speaking of airport runways. *Asphalt* or *blacktop* is the term used for a road surface for automobiles. In the UK, however, *tarmac* is often used when referring to a road surface as well.

- The American and British legal systems are somewhat different. A trial attorney is the rough equivalent of a British *barrister*. In the US, a person can confer directly with a trial attorney. In Britain, you confer with your solicitor, who in turn confers with your barrister. Since 1970 the term *paralegal* has been used in the US for someone trained to perform certain legal tasks for a lawyer. An *articled clerk* performs similar duties in Britain.

- In both countries, some words are mainly written but seldom spoken. In the US if you look through the yellow pages for a car rental agency, you will need to look under *Automobile Rentals,* even though the term *car* is much more common than *automobile.* Similarly, a sign at the side of the road might read *Next Signal: Rose Street,* but in speaking, a person would say "next *light.*" In Britain an equivalent is found in the WC sign. The average Briton does not ask where the WC is (although a foreign visitor might). Instead they might ask where the *loo* is.

- In many US colleges, the first-year course that introduces a particular is given the course designation number 101, as in Physics 101 or Spanish 101. The term *101* is often used in American speech to indicate a basic course in a jocular sense ("He needs to take Etiquette 101").

- Among the words first used in America that have made their way back to Britain are *lasso, moccasin, outlandish, widget,* and the extremely common expression *OK.*

- In speech, Americans sometimes specify the country in which well-known cities are located and say *Paris, France* or *Rome, Italy* rather than just *Paris* or *Rome.* This may be in order to avoid confusion, since many towns in the US have been named after European cities, such as *Athens, Georgia.*

- Some nicknames of American men are not used in Britain, such as *Bud, Buzz, Chip, Chuck, Hank, Butch, Randy* and *Bubba* (this last name is especially associated with the South).

- *Ate:* The pronunciation of *ate* is a little tricky. Americans say this word exactly like *eight.* In Britain one is taught to pronounce it *et.* This is confusing, but if you wish to have a command of English wherever you are, it is necessary to change the way you pronounce *ate.*

- The letters PTO for *Please Turn Over* are often used when writing in Britain. Americans use the words *Over* or *See over,* sometimes with an arrow added to reinforce the meaning. The letters *NB* (from the Latin *nota bene,* "note well") are often used in Britain, particularly in an instruction manual.

- Some expressions that, surprisingly, are used in both countries are *not my cup of tea, in your neck of the woods, it cost a pretty penny* and *penny wise, pound foolish.*

⊰ 15 ⊱

UK–US Lexicon

A plus sign (+) after a term indicates that the term is known in both the United Kingdom and the United States. If this sign is on both the US and UK sides, the difference is purely in customary word usage. A plus sign is not used when the entry on the US side of the column is merely a definition or an explanation of the term rather than an American equivalent, since the explanation will be understood on both sides of the Atlantic.

Brackets indicate the pronunciation of a word. For a complete guide to pronunciation symbols and other signs, see page vi. An asterisk [*] indicates that further information about a term can be found in *Explanations*, pages 220–227. A slash [/] separates two different American equivalents of the same British term. The label *(colloq.)* indicates that the word is used in colloquial speech.

An entry of the form "homey (see *homey* US)" indicates that the word *homey* is used in one sense in the UK but in another in the US. The reader should consult the US–UK lexicon for the American meaning.

All words are nouns unless otherwise indicated. Where confusion may arise the part of speech has been given.

In compiling this lexicon I have come across several brand names that are as common as, or more common than, the generic names. Because the brand names may not be understood in the other country, I found it essential to include these words.

No endorsement is intended—or should be interpreted—by the use of these words.

UK–US Lexicon

UK	US
abattoir	packinghouse/slaughterhouse +
abseil [**ab**·sīl]	rappel
academician	member of an academy (see *academician* US)
advert	ad +
aerial +	antenna +
aeroplane	airplane
afters *(slang)*	dessert
aggro *(colloq.)*	aggravation
agony column	advice column
air-rifle +	BB gun/air gun
airing cupboard*	small closet over the hot-water tank for storing linens
akela (from the name of the leader of the wolf pack in Rudyard Kipling's *The Jungle Book*)	den mother/adult leader of a pack of Cub Scouts
allotments	community gardens
Alsatian (dog)	German shepherd
amenity tip/dump +	landfill
amongst	among +
anorak	parka +
anticlockwise	counterclockwise
appraisal*	evaluation

For a guide to pronunciation symbols and other signs, see page vi.

UK	US
argy-bargy	a lively or disputatious discussion
arse *(vulgar)*	ass
articled clerk	paralegal (similar)
articulated lorry	tractor-trailer truck/semi [**sem**·ī]
assault course (military)	obstacle/confidence course
assessor (insurance)	adjuster
assurance	life insurance
aubergine [**oh**·ber·zheen]	eggplant
autumn +	fall
badge	pin
bailiff (see *bailiff* US)	person appointed by a judge to confiscate personal property
Balaclava	ski mask
banana skin	banana peel
banger (dilapidated car)	heap +
banger (firework)	firecracker
banger (food)	sausage +
bap	hamburger bun
barmy	nutty + (crazy)
barrister	trial lawyer/trial attorney
barrow	pushcart
bash up	beat up +
basin (bathroom)	sink
bat (table tennis)	paddle
bath	bathtub
bathing costume	swimsuit +
baths	public swimming pool +
batty *(slang)*	nuts

UK	US
beach hut	cabana
beak *(slang)*	magistrate/schoolmaster
beaker	mug + (especially a plastic mug)
bedside table	nightstand
bedsitter	efficiency apartment
beefburger	hamburger +
beetroot	beets
bell-boy +	bellhop
berk *(slang)*	idiot
besotted	smitten +
bespoke (clothing)	made to order
billion*	a million million (The US *billion* is a thousand million.)
bin *(verb)*	toss/pitch
bird *(offensive slang)*	girl
Biro (brand name)	ballpoint pen +
bish	screwup
Black Maria +	paddy wagon
bleeper	beeper
blighter *(slang)*	idiot
blind (pull-down)	shade/window shade
blinking *(slang)*	goddamn
block letters	capital letters +
block of flats	apartment building
bloke *(slang)*	guy
bloody *(slang)*	damn
bloomer (mistake)	blooper/boo-boo

For a guide to pronunciation symbols and other signs, see page vi.

UK	US
bobby	cop +
boffin *(colloq.)*	research scientist, egghead (originally World War II slang)
bog *(slang)*	john (toilet)
bogey *(slang)*	booger [bû·ger] *(colloq.)*
boiled sweets	hard candy
boiler (central heating)	furnace
boiler suit	coveralls
bollard*	stanchion/illuminated traffic diverter
bolshy *(slang)*	ornery
bolt-hole	hideaway +
Bonio (brand of dog biscuit)	Milk-Bone (brand name)
bonnet (on a car)	hood
boob (mistake)	boo-boo *(colloq.)*
book token	gift certificate for a book
bookstall	newsstand
boot (on a car)	trunk
booze-up	drinking spree
Borstal	reform school +
bottle (fruit and vegetables) *(verb)*	can*
bottom drawer	hope chest
bottom of (street or garden)	far end of
bowler hat	derby
bowls	lawn bowling
braces	suspenders
bracken	a coarse kind of fern, often growing thickly in patches

UK	US
brainwave	inspiration/great idea
brass *(colloq.)*	money
breeze-block	cinder block
bridge-roll	hotdog bun
brilliant *(slang)*	great/cool
bring up (a child)	raise
broad bean	fava bean [**fah**·və]
brogues (shoes)	oxfords
brooch	pin
brothel-creepers *(slang)*	rubber-soled suede shoes
bucket-shop *(colloq.)*	travel agency selling discount travel tickets (see *bucket shop* US)
buckshee *(slang)*	free/for free
budgerigar +	Australian parakeet
builder	owner of a building company/construction worker
building site	construction site +
bulrush	cattail
bum *(slang)*	butt/fanny/buns
bumbag	fanny pack/belly bag/belt bag
bumf *(colloq.)*	unwanted papers and documents
bun fight *(colloq.)*	bash/party
bung *(slang verb)*	throw
bungalow*	any one-story house
bunk off	play hookey +
bureau	secretary desk
burgle	burglarize
busker	street musician

For a guide to pronunciation symbols and other signs, see page vi.

UK	US
busy Lizzie (flower)	impatiens
butter-bean	lima bean [lie·ma]
buttonhole	boutonniere
cack-handed	awkward, clumsy
camp bed	cot
candyfloss	cotton candy
canteen	cafeteria +
car-boot sale	tailgate sale (not common in the US)
car park	parking lot
caravan	trailer/mobile home
caravan site	trailer park
carer	caregiver
carrier bag	tote bag/shopping bag +
carry-cot	baby carrier
cash machine/cash dispenser	ATM (automatic teller machine)
cashier	teller in a bank or post office (cashier in other businesses)
cashpoint	cash machine/ATM
casket	small ornamental box (see *casket* US)
castor sugar	confectioners' sugar
casualty (hospital)	emergency
catapult +	slingshot
Catherine wheel (firework)	pinwheel
catmint	catnip +
cattle-grid	cattle guard
catwalk (for modeling clothes)	runway
caustic soda	lye
CCF (Combined Cadet Force)	ROTC (Reserve Officers' Training Corps.)

UK	US
central reservation	median/median strip
chap	guy*/fellow +
charity shop	thrift shop
chartered accountant	CPA (certified public accountant)
chartered surveyor	licensed surveyor
chat show	talk show
cheeky	nervy/fresh/sassy
cheerio	goodbye
cheers*	thanks/bye
chemist (person)	pharmacist +
chemist (shop)	drugstore/pharmacy +
chick-pea	garbanzo bean
chicory	endive
chipolata	small sausage
chippings	gravel/small stones
chips	French fries/fries
chivvey (verb)	badger/keep after
choc-ice	Klondike (brand name)
chock-a-block full	chock-full
Christian name	first name/given name
Christmas pudding	plum pudding +
chuffed (colloq.)	delighted
CID (Criminal Investigation Department)	FBI (Federal Bureau of Investigation)
cigarette end	cigarette butt +
cinema +	movie theater
city centre	downtown

For a guide to pronunciation symbols and other signs, see page vi.

UK	US
cladding (on a building)	siding
cling film (plastic food wrap)	Saran Wrap (brand name)
clinker	something admirable or first-rate
cloakroom	restroom/checkroom
clobber (slang)	clothing/equipment
clock (slang)	face
clockwork (of a toy)	wind-up
clod (slang for idiot)	dipstick
(a) close [klohz]	a short dead-end street
cloth-cap (adj.)	blue-collar +
clothes-peg	clothespin
cobble together	patch together +
cockshy	mark aimed at in throwing contests, an object of ridicule
cock-up (noun, slang)	foul-up
codger	old man
cohort	a group of people representing a common cause (see cohort US)
commercial traveller	traveling salesman +
commis waiter	busboy
commissionaire	uniformed doorman
common (adj., of a person)	low-life
common (noun)	public parkland
compère	m.c./master of ceremonies +
concession (when paying for admission)	discount
conjurer	magician +
compulsory purchase	eminent domain

UK	US
conkers	buckeyes (similar to horse chestnuts)/horse chestnuts
conscription	draft
constable	police officer
cooker	range/stove +
copper *(slang)*	cop +
cordial (drink)	nonalcoholic drink made from fruit juice (see *cordial* US)
coriander	cilantro (refers to leaves only; the seeds are called *coriander* in the US)
cornflour	cornstarch
corner shop	convenience store
cornet (for ice cream)	cone +
cornfield*	wheat field
cos lettuce [koss]	romaine lettuce
cosh	club +/nightstick
cot	crib
cottage hospital	country hospital with no resident doctor
cotton swab	Q-Tip (brand name)
cotton wool	cotton
council estate	public housing project
councillor	councilman
courgette [kor·zhet]	zucchini [zoo·kee·nee]
court shoes	pumps (dress shoes for ladies)
covering letter	cover letter
cow gum	rubber cement
cowboy *(slang)*	disreputable workman

For a guide to pronunciation symbols and other signs, see page vi.

UK	US
cowpat	cowpie
crackers *(slang)*	nuts +
cranky	eccentric (see *cranky* US)
crash barrier (on a road)	guardrail
cravat	ascot
crayfish +	crawfish
crazy paving*	patchwork paved surface
cream cracker	soda cracker
create *(verb, slang)*	make a fuss
creek	narrow tidal inlet (see *creek* US)
creeper	vine
crematorium +	crematory [**cree**·ma·tory]
crisps	potato chips
crock *(colloq.)*	worn-out person or thing
crockery	plates and dishes (see *crockery* US)
crosspatch	grouch +
cruet	small container for condiments at the table (see *cruet* US)
crush barrier	barricade +
crust (on the end of a loaf)	heel
CS gas	Mace (brand name)
cubicle (toilet)	stall
cupboard +	cabinet
cuppa *(slang)*	cup of tea
curate	assistant church minister
curate's egg	something with both good and bad qualities
curtains +	drapes/draperies

UK	US
custom (as in *I will never give that shop my custom again*)	business, patronage
cutthroat razor	straight razor
cut up *(colloq.)*	upset/distressed (see *cut-up* US)
cutlery	flatware/silverware
cutting (newspaper)	clipping +
c.v. (curriculum vitae)	resumé (In the US, a c.v. is typically longer than a resumé.)
daft	dumb
dandelion-clock	dandelion flower head
death duties	estate taxes
decorator	house painter +
demerara sugar	brown sugar
diary (for appointments)	calendar
diddle *(verb)*	cheat/swindle
digestive biscuits	graham crackers (similar)
digs *(colloq.)*	student accommodations (see *digs* US)
dinner jacket	tuxedo/tux
dish *(verb)*	ruin, foil, or defeat
dish up	serve
dishy *(colloq.)*	cute
dismantle +	disassemble
disorientated	disoriented
diversion (on a road)	detour
DIY shop	home improvement store
do up	make over/do over
dodgy	uncertain/risky

For a guide to pronunciation symbols and other signs, see page vi.

UK	US
doggo *(colloq.)*	motionless/uncooperative
dogsbody	gofer
(the) dole	unemployment benefits
domestic science	home economics/home ec +
donkey-work	grunt work
doodah	doodad
dormitory	room used for sleeping (see *dormitory* US)
dormitory suburb	bedroom suburb
doss-house	flophouse
dotty	nutty + (crazy)
double saucepan	double boiler +
double-barrelled surname	hyphenated last name
down-and-out *(noun)*	bum
drainpipe +	rainspout/downspout
draper	dry-goods retailer
draughts	checkers
dressing-gown	bathrobe
drink driving	drunk driving
dripping	fat left in the pan after roasting meat
dry goods	foodstuffs (see *dry goods* US)
duds *(slang)*	clothes
dumb waiter*	lazy Susan
dummy (for a baby)	pacifier
dustbin	trash can/garbage can
dustbin day	garbage day
dustcart	garbage truck
dustman	garbage collector
Dutch courage	alcohol-induced courage

UK	US
earth wire	ground wire
eiderdown	comforter
Elastoplast (brand name)	Band-Aid (brand name) +
elevenses	morning tea break
emulsion paint	latex paint
en suite (of a room)	with a bathroom
envisage	envision +
estate agent	realtor*/real-estate agent
estate car	station wagon
evening classes	night school
excess (on insurance)	deductible
expiry date	expiration date
fag *(colloq.)*	cigarette (see *fag* US)
faggot	a traditional English meatball made from pork liver, onions, and bread
fairy cake	cupcake +
fancy *(colloq.)*	feel in the mood for (something)/ be sexually attracted to (a person)
fancy-dress party	costume party
Father Christmas +	Santa Claus +
fender (on a boat) +	bumper
fête [fayt] or [fett]	village fair
film +	movie +
fire (gas/electric)	heater
fire brigade	fire department
fish fingers	fish sticks
fish slice	spatula/pancake turner
fitted carpet	wall-to-wall carpet

For a guide to pronunciation symbols and other signs, see page vi.

UK	US
fixture (sporting)	sporting event +
fizzy drink	pop/soda
flagon (old-fashioned)	jug (see *jug* UK)
flannel	washcloth/facecloth
flannel *(slang)*	BS *(vulgar slang)*/hogwash
flash *(colloq.)*	showy
flask +	thermos +
flat	apartment/condominium/condo
flatmate	roommate
flat out	all out
flautist	flutist
fleapit	a cheap or squalid cinema/movie theater
flex (electrical)	cord
flick-knife	switchblade
flipping *(slang adj.)*	darn
flog *(slang)*	sell
flummox *(colloq.)*	confuse
flutter *(colloq.)*	wager
fly-past	flyover
foot-and-mouth disease +	hoof-and-mouth disease
football	soccer (game)/soccer ball
football pitch	football field
football pools	British gambling consortium with the winnings based on the outcome of certain football matches
footer *(colloq.)*	soccer
footpath	sidewalk/trail
forecourt	area around the gasoline pumps

UK	US
forthcoming	upcoming
fortnight	two weeks
foyer +	lobby +
Freephone/Freefone	toll free
freehold	outright ownership of land
French pleat (hairstyle)	French twist/French roll
fringe (hair)	bangs
frock	dress +
frog-spawn	frogs' eggs
frowsty	having a stale smell/musty
fruit machine	slot machine
fug	stuffy or smoky atmosphere
full marks	full or due credit or praise
full stop (punctuation)	period
further education	continuing education
gammy (leg)	game/injured
garden +	yard*
gasometer	gas-storage facility
gawp *(verb)*	rubberneck
gazump *(colloq.)*	raise the price of real estate after having accepted an offer
gin (alternative meaning)	trap (see *gin* US)
ginger-nut	gingersnap
girl guide	Girl Scout
git *(noun, slang)*	jerk
golden handshake	retirement present (for long service)
good books	good graces
goods lift	freight elevator

For a guide to pronunciation symbols and other signs, see page vi.

UK	US
goose-pimples/goose-flesh	goose bumps +
goosegogs *(colloq.)*	gooseberries
granny flat	mother-in-law apartment
greaseproof paper	wax paper
green card	motorists' international insurance document (see *green card* US)
green fingers	green thumb +
greengage	green plum
greengroceries	produce [**prō**·doos]
greenkeeper	greenskeeper
greens *(slang)*	vegetables
grill +	broil*
grotty *(slang)*	scuzzy +
ground floor	first floor
group litigation order (legal term)	class-action suit
guide dog	Seeing Eye dog
gum-shield	mouth guard
guttering	gutters +
gymkhana	horse show
hair slide	barrette
half-moon glasses	half glasses
handbag +	purse/pocket book
hard graft	laborious work
hardback (book)	hardcover
hash (#)	pound sign
hassock	kneeler/church kneeling cushion (see *hassock* US)
hatch (in a house)	pass-through

UK	US
haulier	person or firm that moves things/hauler +
head waiter	maitre d'
headmaster/headmistress +	principal
heath	open parkland
hedgerow	row of bushes forming a long hedge
hen party	girls' night out
hessian	burlap
het up	agitated
hide (for animal watchers)	blind
hip bag	belt bag
hire* *(verb)*	rent
hire purchase, buy on *(verb)*	make payments/installments on
hive off	separate from/break away from
hoarding	billboard +
hob	range top/stove top
holiday*	vacation
holiday-maker	vacationer
homely*	homey (see *homely* US)
hooter *(slang)*	nose (see *hooters* US)
Hoover (brand name)	vacuum +
horse blinkers	horse blinders
horsebox	horse trailer
horse riding	horseback riding
hot flush	hot flash
hotchpotch	hodgepodge
house builder	homebuilder

For a guide to pronunciation symbols and other signs, see page vi.

UK	US
house-trained	housebroken
housing estate	subdivision
the hump	depression, an emotional slump
ice lolly	Popsicle (brand name)
icing +*	frosting
identity/identification parade	line up +
immersion heater	hot water heater (electric)
indicator (on a car)	turn signal
inheritance tax	estate tax
Inland Revenue	Internal Revenue Service (IRS)
insect +	bug +
inverted commas	quotation marks +
invigilator (at university exams)	proctor (see *proctor* UK)
ironmonger	hardware dealer
jam jar	jelly jar
jammy *(colloq.)*	lucky
jelly	Jell-O (brand name)
jemmy	jimmy
jiggery-pokery *(colloq.)*	trickery
jim-jams *(colloq.)*	jammies
jobber	a middleman in the exchange of stocks and securities among brokers
Jobcentre	employment office
Joe Bloggs	Joe Blow
joiner	cabinetmaker
joint	roast +
jollies *(colloq.)*	laughs/kicks
judder	vibrate and shake

UK	US
jug*	pitcher
jumble sale	rummage sale +
jumper	sweater +
kerfuffle	commotion
kettle +	teakettle
key money	a month's rent plus deposit
kieselguhr	diatomaceous earth +
kiosk +	concession stand
kip *(colloq.)*	sleep
kirby-grip (originally the brand name Kirbigrip)	bobby pin
knacker	someone who buys old horses for slaughter
knacker's yard *(colloq.)*	glue factory
knackered *(slang)*	beat/exhausted
knickerbockers	knickers
knickers	panties
knock up* *(colloq.)*	wake up/warm up (in tennis)/put together (see *knock up* US)
knocking-off time	quitting time
labour exchange (now Jobcentre)	employment office
ladder (in stockings)	run
ladybird	ladybug
larder	pantry +
lashings of *(colloq.)*	gobs of
launderette	laundromat
lavatory +	bathroom/rest room

For a guide to pronunciation symbols and other signs, see page vi.

UK	US
lead (electrical)	cord
lead (for a dog) +	leash +
leading article	editorial
lean-to	a building with a sloping roof abutting a larger building (see *lean-to* US)
leasehold property	property that may be bought and sold but is ultimately owned by another party
leery (glance)	sly/knowing (see *leery* US)
let (property)	lease/rent out
letter-box	mailbox/mail drop
Liberty (humans rights organization)	ACLU (American Civil Liberties Union)
lido	public outdoor swimming pool
lifebelt/lifebuoy	life preserver
lift	elevator
lightning-conductor	lightning rod
Lilo [lie·low] (brand name)	air mattress +
lino [lie·noh] *(colloq.)*	linoleum (originally a brand name)
lipsalve	Chap Stick (brand name)/lip balm
listed building	historic building
litter bin	trash can
Little Bear (constellation)	Little Dipper
liver sausage	liverwurst
local authority	city/county (similar but not an exactly equivalent level of government)
lodger	boarder/roomer

UK	US
loft	attic +
lollipop +	sucker (for children)
long-sighted	farsighted
loo *(slang)*	john
loud-hailer	bullhorn
lounge	family room
lounge suit	business suit +
lovebite	hickey
lucerne	alfalfa +
lucky dip	grab bag
luv *(slang term of endearment)*	hon [hun]
mac/mackintosh	raincoat
mad *(hip slang)*	rad
Madeira cake	pound cake
mailshot	flier (sent through the mail), mass mailing
main course (in a restaurant)	entrée
mains*	main
maisonette	an apartment with a private front door accessible from the exterior (usually in a two-story apartment complex)
maize	corn +
manager (in business)	vice president
managing director (in business)	president/CEO
mange-tout [**mahnzh**·too]	snow peas +
market gardener	truck farmer

For a guide to pronunciation symbols and other signs, see page vi.

UK	US
marks (in school)	grades
marquee*	large tent (see *marquee* US)
marrow	large zucchini
mate *(colloq.)*	man/bud
maths	math
me *(colloq.)*	my
mean	stingy (see *mean* US)
Meccano set (brand name)	Erector set (brand name)
megaphone	bullhorn
mercy flight	medevac flight
methylated spirits/meths	denatured alcohol
midge	gnat +
milk churn	milk can
milk float	milk delivery truck
minced meat	ground meat
mincer	meat grinder
mind *(verb)*	watch for/look out for
Mind the Gap! (sign and automated announcement in the London Underground subway system)	Watch your step! (when exiting or boarding the train)
mobile (phone)	cell (phone)
momentarily	for a moment (see *momentarily* US)
mortise lock	dead bolt
mount (around a picture)	mat
mouth organ	harmonica +
mozzie (*slang* for *mosquito*)	skeeter (*slang*, regional South)
muck about *(colloq.)*	cut up
muck in *(colloq.)*	pitch in

UK	US
mudguard	fender
mug up	bone up
multi-storey car park	parking garage
mum	mom
music hall	vaudeville
musical box	music box
mutt *(slang)*	dog (see *mutt* US)
NAAFI (Navy, Army, and Airforce Institutes)	PX (Post Exchange) (similar organization)
naff	unstylish, outmoded, worthless
nail varnish	nail polish +
nappy	diaper
narkey *(slang)*	irritable
natty	spiffy
navvy	laborer on a public project
neat (of a drink)	straight
nervy	nervous (see *nervy* US)
net curtains	sheer curtains/sheers
New Year's Eve	New Year's *(colloq.)*
newsagent	newspaper store/newsstand +
newsreader	newscaster
nick *(slang)*	steal
nightdress	nightgown
nil	zip/zero +
nipper *(colloq.)*	kid/young shaver
Nissen hut (trademark)	Quonset hut (trademark)
nod *(colloq.)*	big shot

For a guide to pronunciation symbols and other signs, see page vi.

UK	US
noddle	noodle +
normal/usual +	regular
nosey parker *(slang)*	busybody
nosh up *(slang)*	feast
note (currency)	bill
notice-board	bulletin board
noughts and crosses	tic-tac-toe
number-plate	license plate
o.n.o. (or near offer)	o.b.o. (or best offer)
OAP (old age pensioner)	senior citizen +
oblique (the/symbol)	slash +
off-licence	liquor store
off-putting	deterring
oik	hood/lout +
old age pension	Social Security (see *social security* UK)
one-off	custom-made
ordinary shares	common stock
outhouse	shed near or next to a house (see *outhouse* US)
outsize	extra-large +
overspill	movement of people from overcrowded cities to less populated areas
overtake (a car on a road) +	pass +
P&P (postage and packing)	S&H (shipping and handling)
P.T.O. (please turn over)	(over)
pack (of cards) +	deck
paddle (walk through shallow water)	wade +

UK	US
paddling pool	wading pool
palaver [pə·**lah**·ver]	commotion
panda car	police cruiser
pantomime	theatrical Christmas performance (see *pantomime* US)
paper round	paper route
paraffin	kerosene
paralytic *(slang)*	wasted/very drunk
parky (regional North)	chilly
parting (in hair)	part
patience (card game)	solitaire (see *solitaire* UK)
pavement	sidewalk (see *pavement* US)
pavilion (alternative meaning)	main building on a sports field
paving-stone	concrete slab/paver
pawky	shrewd and cunning, often in a humorous manner
peaky	peaked [**pee**·kid]
pebble-dash	pebble-coated stucco
peckish *(colloq.)*	hungry
pelmet	cornice/valance (see *valance* UK)
pelt down (with rain)	bucket down
pen-friend	pen pal
penny-farthing (type of bicycle)	high wheeler
pensioner	senior citizen +
Perspex (brand name)	Plexiglas (brand name)
petrol	gas/gasoline
phonograph	early phonograph using cylinders (see *phonograph* US)

For a guide to pronunciation symbols and other signs, see page vi.

UK	US
physiotherapist	physical therapist
Pianola (brand name)	player piano
(the) pictures	movies
piffle	nonsense/garbage
pillar-box	mailbox
pin	straight pin (in New England a *common pin*)
pinafore dress	jumper
pinch *(slang)*	steal
pip	seed/pit (in fruit)
pissed *(vulgar slang)*	drunk (see *pissed* US)
pitch (sporting term)	field +
pith	pulp
plait	braid
planning permission	permit
plaster (for a wound)	Band-Aid (brand name) +
Plasticine (brand name)	Play-Doh (brand name)
play up	act up +
plimsolls	canvas sneakers
plonk *(slang)*	cheap wine
plot +	lot +
Plough (constellation)	Big Dipper
pneumatic drill +	jackhammer
podgy	pudgy
point (to add mortar to brickwork)	tuck-point
polisher (electric)	buffer
polo-neck	turtleneck
Polyfilla (brand name)	Spackle (brand name)

UK	US
polystyrene	Styrofoam (brand name)
pong	stink +
pontoon (card game)	blackjack +
poppet	dear, darling
porridge	oatmeal (cooked)
post +*	mail +
post-mortem +	autopsy +
postcode	Zip Code
postie	mailman/postman
pot plant	potted plant/houseplant
potholer	spelunker (cave explorer)
potter (around)	putter
pouffe	hassock/ottoman
power point	electrical outlet
pram/perambulator	baby carriage/stroller
prat	fool
prawns +	shrimp +
prefect (in a school)	monitor +
presently	soon +
press-studs	snaps (fasteners)
press-ups	pushups +
primary school	grammar school/grade school
prise open	pry open
prison warder	corrections officer
proctor	disciplinary officer at a university (see *proctor* US)
produce [**prŏd**·yoos]	all agricultural products (see *produce* US)

For a guide to pronunciation symbols and other signs, see page vi.

UK	US
propelling pencil	mechanical pencil
property	real estate
prospectus	brochure (*prospectus* is only used for finances in the US)
proud (as in *proud flesh*)	projecting slightly above, swollen, overgrown
pub	bar +
public prosecutor	district attorney/DA
public telephone box	pay phone +
public transport	public transportation
pudding basin	pudding bowl +
pumps	canvas sneakers
puncture	flat (tire)
punnet	container for fruit or vegetables
punter	customer/someone who bets on horses/prostitute's client
purse	change purse
push-bike	bicycle +
pushchair	stroller
put-you-up	sofa bed/Hide-A-Bed (brand name)
pylon	high-tension tower
quay [kee]	wharf +
query *(verb)*	question
queue up	line up
quid *(slang)*	pound (money)
quieten down	quiet down
rabbit on *(verb, colloq.)*	rattle on +
racecourse +	racetrack
rag *(verb, colloq.)*	razz

UK	US
rag *(noun)*	newspaper
railway	railroad
ramble	hike +
randy *(slang)*	frisky/sexually aroused
rasher	slice of bacon +
rates	property taxes
ratty *(colloq.)*	irritable (see *ratty* US)
redcap *(colloq.)*	MP (a member of the military police) (see *redcap* US)
redundancies	layoffs
reef-knot	square knot
reel of cotton	spool of thread
registrar (legal and university)	senior administrative officer
removal van	moving van
restaurant car	dining car
retirement pension	Social Security
return ticket	round-trip ticket
reverse-charge call	collect call
ride-on mower	riding mower
ring up (phone)	call
rise (in pay)	raise
road surface +	pavement
rock/seaside rock	stick candy
rockery	rock garden
rota	roster +
round (delivery)	route
roundabout (for children)	merry-go-round

For a guide to pronunciation symbols and other signs, see page vi.

UK	US
roundabout (traffic)	traffic circle/rotary (New England)
rowlock [rŏ·lŏk]	oarlock
royal *(slang adj.)*	fabulous +
RSPCA (Royal Society for the Prevention of Cruelty to Animals)	ASPCA (American Society for the Prevention of Cruelty to Animals)/ SPCA (Society for the Prevention of Cruelty to Animals)
rubber	eraser
rubbish	garbage/trash
Rubbish!	Nonsense!
ruddy *(slang adj.)*	darn
rug (light blanket)*	throw
rumbustious	rambunctious
rumpus +	ruckus
runner beans	string beans
sack *(verb)*	fire/can
saddle (on a bicycle)	seat
(on) sale*	for sale
saleroom	salesroom
sales talk	sales pitch
saloon bar	lounge bar +
salt beef	corned beef
sandpit	sandbox
sandwich-cake	layer cake
sanitary towel	sanitary napkin
sapper	British soldier specializing in rebuilding destroyed structures
saucy	impudent/sassy
scarper	run away

UK	US
scatty	scatterbrained
scheme (financial)	plan +
scone	biscuit
screw (*slang*)	prison guard
scribbling block	scratch paper
scrum	scrimmage (in sports); confusion
scrump *(verb)*	steal fruit off trees
scrumpy	locally made, rough hard cider (contains alcohol)
scullery	room off a kitchen for washing dishes
scupper	ruin, destroy
seaside	beach +
secateurs	pruners/pruning shears
secondary glazing	storm window
self-raising flour	self-rising flour
Sellotape (brand name)	Scotch tape (brand name)
semi-detached (house)	duplex* (similar)
semolina	Cream of Wheat (brand name)
send up	imitate/ridicule
service flats	apartment hotel
serviette	napkin +
settee +	couch/sofa +
shambolic	in a shambles/disorderly/chaotic
shandy	a drink that is half beer and half lemonade
sheltered accommodation	assisted-living facility/ALF
sheriff	a person who performs public duties similar to a mayor (see *sheriff* US)

For a guide to pronunciation symbols and other signs, see page vi.

UK	US
shin-pad	shin guard
shin up +	shinny up
shingle*	beach pebbles (see *shingle* US)
shirty	irritable
shoeblack	bootblack
shop *(colloq.)*	turn in to the authorities
shop assistant	salesperson
shop steward	labor union representative
shopping centre +	mall*
shopping trolley	shopping cart
shop-soiled merchandise	display merchandise
short-sighted (vision)	nearsighted
sideboards	sideburns +
sidesman	usher (in a church)
simnel	Easter fruitcake with marzipan
single ticket	one-way ticket
singlet	men's sleeveless undershirt
skint (*slang*, as in *I'm skint*)	broke +
skip *(noun)*	Dumpster (brand name)
skip *(verb)*	jump rope
skipping-rope *(noun)*	jump rope
skirting-board	baseboard
skive off *(verb)*	play hookey +
skivvy	female servant performing menial tasks
slate *(colloq.)*	criticize (see *slate* US)
sleeping partner	silent partner
slice/fish slice	spatula/pancake turner

UK	US
slim *(verb)*	slim down/diet +
Sloanes/Sloane Rangers *(slang)*	yuppies (usually Londoners)
slops	cheap, ready-made garments
slot machine	vending machine + (see *slot machine* US)
small print +	fine print +
smalls *(colloq.)*	underwear
smashing	awesome/cool/neat
snagging list	punch list (construction)
snakes and ladders (game)	Chutes and Ladders (brand name)
sneak *(noun)*	tattle-tale
snip *(noun)*	bargain/deal
snog *(slang)*	kiss amorously
snuggery	snug position or place
social security	welfare (see *Social Security* US)
sod *(vulgar)*	son of a bitch
soft drink +	soda/pop/tonic (in Boston)/Coke (in the South)
soil +	dirt
solicitor	lawyer/attorney
solitaire	peg solitaire (see *solitaire* US)
soppy	sappy
sort code	routing number
sous chef	commis chef
soya beans	soybeans
spanner	wrench +
speciality	specialty

For a guide to pronunciation symbols and other signs, see page vi.

UK	US
spectacles +	glasses +/eyeglasses
spitting (rain)	sprinkling +
spiv	small-time operator/shyster
spod	someone who spends an inordinate amount of time in computer chatrooms, newsgroups, or bulletin boards
sponge bag	toilet bag
sports jacket	sport coat
spot of	small amount of
spring onion	green onion/scallion
squash (orange)	fruit concentrate mixed with water
stabilisers (on a child's bike)	training wheels
Stanley knife (brand name)	utility knife
state school	public school
STD (subscriber trunk dialling)	long distance (see STD US)
stick beans	pole beans
sticker +	decal [dee·cal] or [de·cal]
still (of a beverage)	noncarbonated
stirrer (colloq.)	troublemaker
stockings +	hose
stockist	commercial retailer or wholesaler that stocks merchandise
stone (in fruit)	pit
stone (unit of weight)	fourteen pounds
stopover +	layover
straight away	immediately +
stream	course of study to which students are tracked

UK	US
Strimmer (brand of grass trimmer)	Weed Whacker (brand name)
stroke (the / symbol)	slash +
stroppy	easily offended or annoyed, ill-tempered or belligerent
stuffing +	dressing
subsidence (in the ground)	depression/settling
subway	underpass
sultanas	white or golden raisins
summer time	daylight-saving time
sundowner	drink taken at sundown
superannuation	pension plan
supply teacher	substitute teacher
surgery	room where a doctor sees his patients
surname +	last name +
survey *(verb)*	inspect and determine the structural condition of (a building)
suspenders	garters
suss out *(colloq.)*	scope out/figure out
swallow dive	swan dive
swan	travel around from place to place
swede	rutabaga [**roo**·ta·bā·gə]
sweet	dessert +
sweets	candy
swipe *(slang)*	steal
swish *(colloq.)*	fancy/elaborate
Swiss roll	jelly roll

For a guide to pronunciation symbols and other signs, see page vi.

UK	US
swizz	scam/disappointment
swot up (on)	bone up on/study up on
ta *(slang)*	thanks
ta-ta *(slang)*	goodbye
table *(verb)*	bring forward for discussion at a meeting (see *table* US)
take-away (food)	takeout
tap	faucet
tarmac (on a road)	blacktop
tart *(vulgar slang)*	female prostitute/hooker *(vulgar slang)*
teatime	late afternoon
tea towel	dishtowel/kitchen towel
teat (on a baby's bottle)	nipple
tell-tale *(noun, adj.)*	tattletale
telly *(slang)*	TV +
terraced house	row house
terraces (at a sporting event)	stands +
Territorial Army	Reservists
third-party insurance	liability insurance
tick off	reprimand (see *tick off* US)
tick over	idle/operate at a minimal level
tick *(noun)*	check mark
tick *(verb)*	check
tiffin	meal at midday, a luncheon
tights	pantyhose
till +	cash register +
timber	lumber

UK	US
tin	can
tin-opener	can opener +
tip	dump +
Tippex (brand name)	Wite-Out (brand name)
tit (bird)	chickadee
titbit	tidbit
toady (colloq.)	brownnoser (vulgar)
toboggan*	sled
toerag	jerk
toffee apple	candy apple
toffee-nosed (slang)	stuck-up
togs (colloq.)	clothes
toilet	rest room/bathroom/men's room/ women's room
tombola	ticket lottery held at a fair
top up (for a drink)	top off/freshen
torch	flashlight
tortoiseshell cat	calico cat (similar)
tot up	add up +
tout (noun)	scalper
towards +	toward
tower block	high-rise +
trading estate	industrial park
traffic fine	ticket
traffic warden	parking enforcement officer
trainers	sneakers
tram	streetcar
tramp +	bum/hobo

For a guide to pronunciation symbols and other signs, see page vi.

UK	US
transfer +	decal [**dee**·cal]
trapezium	trapezoid
trapezoid	trapezium
travelling party	progressive dinner
treacle	molasses
tread in (dirt)	track in
tread on +	step on +
trilby (hat)	fedora
tripper	someone taking a short pleasure trip
trolley	cart
trousers +	pants +
trug	a shallow gardening basket
truncheon	billy club/nightstick
trunk + (large suitcase)	steamer trunk
tube (train)	subway
tuck in (to food)	dig in +
tuition	tutoring/teaching
tumble-drier	dryer
turf +	sod +
turn-ups (on trousers)	cuffs
turnip-tops	turnip greens
turtle-neck	crew neck
twee	excessively dainty
twig *(colloq.)*	catch on/realize
twister *(colloq.)*	swindler (see *twister* US)
tyre lever +	tire wrench/tire iron
undercarriage (on a plane)	landing gear
undercut (a cut of meat)	beef tenderloin, fillet

UK	US
underground (train)	subway
unit trust (financial)	mutual fund
upfield (in sports)	downfield
upmarket	upscale
valance (on a bed)	dust ruffle/bed skirt (see *valance* US)
valet (a car) *(verb)*	detail
valuer	appraiser*
valves (electronic)	tubes
verge (on a road)	shoulder +/side median
vest	undershirt
veterinary surgeon*	veterinarian
vicar	minister +
video	VCR/videotape
visiting card	calling card
voluntary work	volunteer work
VSO (Voluntary Service Overseas)	Peace Corps
waistcoat	vest
walking-stick +	cane
warder	prison officer/guard
wash up	wash the dishes (see *wash up* US)
water biscuit	soda cracker
water pistol +	squirt gun
way out (on a sign)	exit
WC	restroom
weatherboard	clapboard
wedding ring +	wedding band

For a guide to pronunciation symbols and other signs, see page vi.

UK	US
weir (in a river)	low dam
Wellingtons	rubber boots +
wet *(colloq.)*	sappy
whacked *(slang)*	whipped/beat
whacking *(slang)*	very large
whilst	while +
whinge *(verb, slang)*	bitch
whip-round	collection (usually in an office)
white goods	household appliances
white horses (on waves)	whitecaps
white spirit	liquid solvent
wind (flatulence)	gas
wind [wĭnd] *(verb)*	burp (a baby)
windcheater	windbreaker
windscreen	windshield
winkle out *(verb)*	pry out
witness box	witness stand
wodge	a large amount of something
wonky *(colloq.)*	unstable
woolly	sweater +
worktop (kitchen)	counter/countertop
yard*	paved area around a house (see *yard* US)
yeti	Bigfoot (similar)
yob/yobbo	hood/lout +
zebra crossing [zĕ·bra]	crosswalk/pedestrian crossing +
zip *(noun)*	zipper

⇥ 16 ⇤

US–UK Lexicon

A plus sign [+] after a term indicates that the term is known in both the United Kingdom and the United States. If this sign is on both the US and UK sides, the difference is purely in customary word usage. A plus sign is not used when the entry on the UK side of the column is merely a definition or an explanation of the term rather an American equivalent, since the explanation will be understood on both sides of the Atlantic.

Brackets indicate the pronunciation of a word. For a complete guide to pronunciation symbols, see page vi. An asterisk [*] indicates that further information about a term can be found in Explanations, pages 220–227. A slash [/] separates two different British equivalents of the same American term. The label *(colloq.)* indicates that the word is colloquial. Many Americans may not be familiar with all the slang or colloquial words listed.

An entry of the form "crockery (see *crockery* UK)" indicates that the word *crockery* is used in one sense in the US but in another in the UK. The reader should consult the UK–US lexicon for the British meaning.

All words are nouns unless otherwise indicated. Where confusion may arise the part of speech has been given.

In compiling this lexicon I have come across several brand names that are as common as, or more common than, the generic names. Because the brand names may not be understood in the other country, I found it essential to include these words. No endorsement is intended—or should be interpreted—by the use of these words.

US–UK Lexicon

US	UK
accommodations	accommodation
ace (*verb, colloq.*)	defeat an opponent
ACLU (American Civil Liberties Union)	Liberty (a similar organization)
adjuster (insurance)	assessor
administration (alt. meaning)	government
adobe [ə·**doh**·bee]	brick made from mud and straw
afghan	crocheted or knitted blanket or shawl
airplane	aeroplane
ALF (Assisted Living Facility)	sheltered accommodation
alfalfa +	lucerne
alternate [**alt**·er·net] (*adj.*)	substitute +
Amtrak (stands for *American Travel by Track*)	American passenger-train system
antebellum	pre-Civil War (1861)
antenna +	aerial +
antsy (*slang*)	restless/agitated
anyplace (*colloq.*)	anywhere
anyways (*colloq.*)	anyway
apartment (for rent)	flat (to let)
apartment building	block of flats
apartment hotel	service flats

For a guide to pronunciation symbols and other signs, see page vi.

US	UK
applejack	liquor distilled from fermented cider
appraisal*	valuation
armoire	large, ornate wardrobe
ascot	cravat
ASPCA (American Society for the Prevention of Cruelty to Animals)/SPCA (Society for the Prevention of Cruelty to Animals)	RSPCA (Royal Society for the Prevention of Cruelty to Animals)
ATM (automatic teller machine)	cash machine/cash dispenser
attaboy *(noun, slang)*	commendation
attitude *(slang)*	uncooperative disposition
attorney	lawyer +/solicitor/barrister
autopsy +	post-mortem +
auxiliary (alternative meaning)	an organization of volunteers
awesome *(hip slang)*	mad/brilliant
baby carriage	pram/perambulator
back talk	backchat
badmouth	criticize someone
bag lady	female tramp
bailiff	person who keeps order in a courtroom (see *bailiff* UK)
baloney *(slang)*	codswallop
banana peel	banana skin
bangs (on hair)	fringe
bankroll *(verb)*	give financial support
banner (year)	outstanding
barber +	men's hairdresser +

For a guide to pronunciation symbols and other signs, see page vi.

US	UK
barf *(slang)*	vomit
barrel along *(colloq.)*	belt along
barrette	hair slide
barrio *(colloq.)*	Spanish-speaking district of a town
baseboard	skirting board
bassinet	crib
bathtub	bath
bathrobe	dressing gown
bathroom (in a public building)	toilet/lavatory
bayou (regional South)	marshy inlet
BB gun/air gun	air rifle +
beat *(slang)*	whacked
bedroom suburb	dormitory suburb
bee (as in *spelling bee*)	a meeting held to work or compete with others
beeper	bleeper
beets	beetroot
bellhop	bell-boy +
belt bag	bumbag
benefits (job)	health insurance/pension
Big Dipper (constellation)	Plough
bikini*	men's or women's brief swimsuit
billboard +	hoarding
billfold	notecase/wallet
bills (currency)	notes
billy club/nightstick	truncheon
birder	bird-watcher +
biscuit (the kind served with gravy)	(a quickbread similar to a) scone

US	UK
bitch *(verb, slang)*	whinge
blacktop (on a road)	tarmac
blah	drab
bleachers	terraces/stands +
blind (for animal watchers)	hide
block	the distance between streets in a city
block party	neighborhood party with the street closed to traffic
blooper (mistake)	bloomer
blotter	report of police arrests
blowout (alternative meaning)*	a big party
boarder +	lodger
boardwalk	wooden walkway
bobby pin	flat hairpin
bodacious *(colloq.)*	outstanding
bombed *(colloq.)*	failed +
bone up on	swot up (on)
bone wrench	box spanner
boo-boo *(colloq., for mistake)*	boob
booger [**bû**·ger] *(colloq.)*	bogey *(slang)*
boondocks/boonies *(slang)*	the back of beyond
boot camp	military-style basic training camp
bootblack	shoeblack
box cutter	a thin type of Stanley knife
braid (hair)	plait
branch water	plain water (not carbonated)
break *(colloq.)*	reduction/discount

For a guide to pronunciation symbols and other signs, see page vi.

US	UK
break down (alternative meaning)	give in/relent
breeze (an easy task)	cinch +
breezeway	covered outdoor passageway
brochure (for institutions)	prospectus
broil*	grill +
brown-bagger	someone who takes a homemade lunch to work
brownstone	a terraced house, fronted with sandstone
bubbler (regional North)	drinking fountain +
buck *(colloq.)*	dollar
bucket shop *(colloq.)*	disreputable high-pressure brokerage firm (see *bucket-shop* UK)
buckeyes (seeds of trees like the horse-chestnut)	conkers
buffalo *(colloq.)*	confuse someone for gain
buffer (electric)	polisher
bug +	insect +
building site	vacant lot for building on (see *building site* UK)
bulletin board	notice-board
bullhorn	loud-hailer
bum	tramp
bum *(adj., colloq.* as in *bum leg, bum steer)*	bad
bumper (on a boat)	fender +
bunch of	heap of
bungalow*	small, plain one-storey house
buns *(slang)*	bum
burbs *(slang)*	suburbs

US	UK
bureau	chest of drawers
burglarize	burgle
burlap	hessian
burro	donkey used as a pack animal
busboy/busser	waiter's assistant/commis waiter
bushed	knackered
business suit +	lounge suit
busted *(slang)*	broken +
butt *(slang)*	bum *(slang)*
button* (with a message)	badge
buzz saw	circular saw
cabana	beach hut
cabinet	cupboard +
cabinetmaker	joiner
café	coffee-shop/nightclub
Cajun	pertaining to the people of southern Louisiana who came from Acadia
calendar (for appointments)	diary
calico cat	tortoiseshell cat (similar)
call (phone) +	ring up
calling card	visiting card
calliope [ka·**lie**·ow·pee]	steam organ
can (metal container)	tin
can (toilet)	loo
can *(verb, slang)*	sack
can opener +	tin-opener
can* (in a Mason jar) *(verb)*	bottle (in a Kilner jar)
candy	sweets

For a guide to pronunciation symbols and other signs, see page vi.

US	UK
candy apple	toffee apple
candy striper	young volunteer in a hospital
cane	walking-stick
card (someone) *(verb)*	check someone's age by means of an ID card
caregiver	carer
carnival	funfair
cart (that is pushed)	trolley
cash wrap	counter (in a shop)
casket	coffin + (see *casket* UK)
cathouse *(vulgar slang)*	brothel
catnip	catmint
cattail	bulrush +
cattle guard	cattle-grid
catty-corner/kitty-corner	diagonally across
CD (certificate of deposit)	savings certificate
cell phone	mobile phone
CEO (chief executive officer)	managing director
chalkboard	blackboard +
change purse	purse
chaparral (regional Southwest)	tangled brushwood
Chap Stick (brand name)	lipsalve
charley horse	cramp (in a limb)
licensed surveyor	chartered surveyor
check (in a restaurant)	bill
check mark *(noun)*	tick
check *(verb)*	tick
checker	cashier in a supermarket
checkers	draughts

185

US	UK
checkroom	cloakroom
cherry picker *(colloq.)*	hydraulic boom on a truck that raises a person in the air
chew out *(colloq.)*	scold/reprimand
chickadee	tit (bird)
chigger	harvest mite
chinook [shi·**nûk**]	a warm dry wind on the eastern slopes of the Rocky Mountains/a warm moist wind blowing in from the sea in the Northwest of the US
chipper	chirpy
chopper *(colloq.)* +	helicopter
Chutes and Ladders (game)	snakes and ladders
CIA (Central Intelligence Agency)	espionage bureau
cilantro (refers to leaves only; the seeds are called *coriander*)	coriander
cinder block	breeze-block
circular file *(slang)*	waste-paper basket
clapboard	weatherboard
class-action suit (legal term)	group litigation order
clear across *(colloq.)*	all the way across
clinker	failure
Clorox (brand name)	bleach +
closet	cupboard +
clothespin	clothes-peg
clunker *(colloq.)*	old bomb
co-ed *(colloq.)*	female undergraduate at an educational institution for both men and women

For a guide to pronunciation symbols and other signs, see page vi.

US	UK
coffee *(colloq.)*	social gathering where coffee is served
coffee klatsch	coffee group +
cohort	colleague/supporter (see *cohort* UK)
college (as in phrase *in college*)	university or other college
Colonial	pertaining to the period when Britain ruled the original 13 colonies
comedic (evoking laughter)	comical +
comforter	duvet
commissary (military)	general store
commode *(colloq.)*	toilet
complected	complexioned
concertmaster	leading first violin player
concession stand	snack bar/kiosk +
condominium*/condo	flat
confidence course (military)	assault course
continuing education	further education
cookout	barbecue party
cool* *(slang)*	super/brilliant
cooler	insulated box for keeping food cool
cooties	lice
cordial (drink)	liqueur (see *cordial* UK)
corn (the grain)	maize
corned beef	salt beef
cornice	pelmet
cornstarch	cornflour
corrections officer	prison warder
costume party	fancy-dress party

US	UK
costumer	costumier
cot	camp-bed
cotton	cotton wool
cotton candy	candyfloss
coulee (regional West)	deep ravine
councilman	councillor
counterclockwise	anticlockwise
countertop (kitchen)	worktop
cover letter	covering letter
coveralls	boiler suit
coyote [kie·**oh**·tee]	wild wolflike animal
CPA (certified public accountant)	chartered accountant
crack *(verb, colloq.)**	open slightly (window or door)
cranky	irritable (see *cranky* UK)
crawfish	crayfish +
crazy bone (regional)	funny-bone +
crazy quilt*	patchwork quilt
cream *(slang)*	smash up/beat up
Cream of Wheat (brand name)	semolina
creamer	cream jug
creek	stream (see *creek* UK)
crib	cot (see *cot* US)
critter	a wild animal
crockery (see *crockery* UK)	earthenware pots
crosswalk	pedestrian crossing +
crotch (body part) +	crutch
crud *(slang)*	grime +

For a guide to pronunciation symbols and other signs, see page vi.

US	UK
cruet	glass bottle for vinegar (see *cruet* UK)
cuffs (on pants)	turn-ups
cuss *(slang)*	swear/curse +
cut up *(noun, colloq.)*	joker/buffoon
cut up *(verb, colloq.)*	muck about (see *cut up* UK)
DA	district attorney
darndest	craziest
davenport	large sofa
daylight-saving time	summer time
DC	Washington, DC
deadbeat	someone who is always in debt
dead-bolt	mortise lock
deadhead *(verb)*	to travel without a payload
debark	disembark +
decal [**dee**·cal] or [dee·**cal**]	transfer/sticker +
deck (of a house or building)	paved area or wooden platform adjacent to a house or building
deck (of cards)	pack
deductible (insurance)	excess
den mother	akela [ah·**keh**·lə]/Cub Scout leader
denatured alcohol	methylated spirits/meths
deputy/deputy sheriff	county police officer
derby (rhymes with *herby* in the US)	bowler hat
desk clerk	receptionist
dessert +	pudding/sweet
detail (a car) *(verb)*	valet
detour	diversion

US	UK
diaper [**die**·per]	nappy
diatomaceous earth +	kieselguhr
dicker	haggle/bargain
diddle around *(colloq.)*	fiddle around/waste time
digs *(colloq.)*	accommodation (see *digs* UK)
dirt (as in a yard)	soil +
dis *(verb, hip slang)*	disrespect/snub
disassemble*	dismantle +
discombobulated *(slang)*	disconcerted
dishtowel	tea towel
dishpan	washing-up bowl
dishrag	dishcloth +
disoriented	disorientated
district attorney/DA	public prosecutor
ditsy *(colloq.)*/ditzy	muddleheaded
docent	guide in a museum/lecturer
dog *(colloq.)*	nasty person
dog tag	soldier's identification tag
doghouse	kennel +
doodad	doodah
doohickey	small mechanical object
(a) doozie *(slang)*	something outstanding or overwhelming
dork *(slang)*	idiot
dormitory	building used for sleeping (see *dormitory* UK)
double date	date on which two couples go out for enjoyment together

For a guide to pronunciation symbols and other signs, see page vi.

US	UK
double header	two games played back to back
double saucepan	double boiler
down spout	drainpipe +
(a) downer	something depressing
downfield (in sports)	upfield
downtown	city centre
draft (as in *draft dodger*)	conscription
drag *(verb, colloq.)*	race cars, as in a drag race
drapes/draperies*	curtains
dresser	chest of drawers
dressing (food)	stuffing +
drool +	slobber +
drugstore	chemist/pharmacy +
drunk driving	drink driving
dry goods	fabrics and clothing (see *dry goods* UK)
dude ranch	cattle ranch for holiday-makers
dumb *(slang)*	daft
dummy	twit
Dumpster (brand name)	skip
duplex*	semi-detached house
dust ruffle	valance (see *valance* US)
eavestrough (regional North)	gutter +
Ebonics (from the words *ebony* and *phonics*)	any of the varieties of English spoken by many African-American communities in the US
editorial	leading article
efficiency apartment	bedsitter/bedsit
eggplant	aubergine [oh·ber·zheen]
elevator	lift

US	UK
emergency (room in hospital)	A and E/Accident and Emergency
eminent domain	compulsory purchase
endive	chicory
english (on a pool ball) (regional)	sidespin
envision +	envisage
eraser	rubber
Erector set (brand name)	Meccano set (brand name)
evaluation	appraisal*
expiration date	expiry date
eye candy *(slang)*	something or someone visually appealing
eyeglasses	spectacles/glasses +
facecloth	flannel
facility	building built for a specific purpose
factor in *(verb)*	take into account
fall	autumn +
family room	lounge
fanny *(slang)*	bum *(slang)*
fanny pack *(colloq.)*	bumbag
farsighted	long-sighted
faucet	tap
fava bean [**fah**·və]	broad bean
favor *(verb,* regional South)	to look like +
FBI (Federal Bureau of Investigation)	CID (Criminal Investigation Department)
fedora (hat)	trilby
felony	arrestable offense (similar though not exactly the same)

For a guide to pronunciation symbols and other signs, see page vi.

US	UK
fever blister	cold sore +
fifth	a bottle of liquor, formerly containing a fifth of a gallon (757 ml) but now often containing 750 ml
fill out (a form) +	fill in
fine print +	small print +
fire department	fire brigade
firehouse	fire station +
fire truck	fire engine +
fire *(verb)*	sack
firecracker	banger
first floor	ground floor
fish sticks	fish fingers
fixing to (regional South)	intending to/about to
fixings *(slang)*	trimmings
flashlight	torch
flat (tire)	puncture
flatware	cutlery
flip-flop *(colloq.)*	backward somersault
floor lamp	standard lamp
flophouse	doss-house
flunk *(slang)*	fail
flutist	flautist +
flyover (aircraft)	fly-past
food stamps	coupons that can be exchanged for groceries (given to the needy)
football field	football pitch
foul-up *(noun)*	cock-up

US	UK
fourth	quarter +
frappe (regional New England)	milk shake
freeloader *(colloq.)*	sponger
freight elevator	goods lift
French doors	French windows +
French fries	chips
French twist (hairstyle)	French pleat
fries	chips
frigging (*slang*)	flipping
frogs' eggs	frog-spawn
frosting*	icing +
funky (of an odor)	stinky
furnace (central heating)	boiler
gander + *(slang)*	dekko
garage sale*	jumble sale/rummage sale
garbage	rubbish/kitchen waste
garbage can	dustbin
garbage day	dustbin day
garbage truck	dustcart
garbanzo bean	chickpea +
garters	suspenders
gas (flatulence)	wind
gasoline/gas	petrol
geek *(hip slang)*	dull, studious person
German shepherd	Alsatian
GI (thought to come from *government issue*)	an enlisted person in the US military forces, especially a soldier in the US army

For a guide to pronunciation symbols and other signs, see page vi.

US	UK
gin (as in *cotton gin*)	a machine for separating cotton from its seeds (see *gin* UK)
ginger snap	ginger nut
Girl Scout	Girl Guide
girls' night out	hen party
given name	Christian name
glue factory *(colloq.)*	knacker's yard
goddamn *(slang)*	bloody/blinking
gofer/gopher	general dogsbody
golden raisins	sultanas
golfing knickers	plus-fours +
goof off *(colloq.)*	slack off
goose bumps +	goose-pimples/goose-flesh
gouge/price gouging	overprice
grab bag	lucky dip
grade school	primary school
graham crackers	digestive biscuits (similar)
grammar school	primary school
grandfather clause	exemption because of preexisting circumstances
grandstand *(verb)*	act in a showy way to sway an audience
grease monkey *(slang)*	car mechanic
great room	combined living and dining area
green *(slang)*	money
green card	US permanent-resident card (see *green card* UK)
green onion	spring onion
greenback *(slang)*	dollar bill

US	UK
greenskeeper	greenkeeper
gridiron (sporting term)	football field
grocery store	supermarket +
gross *(slang)*	disgusting
ground meat	minced meat
ground wire	earth wire
groundhog	woodchuck
grunt work *(colloq.)*	donkey-work
guardrail (on a road)	crash barrier
gubernatorial	pertaining to a state governor
guess *(verb,* as in *I guess so)*	suppose/imagine +
gulch	ravine with seasonal water flow
gurney	stretcher on wheels
half-and-half	single cream
half glasses	half-moon glasses
hard candy	boiled sweets
hardcover	hardback
hassock	pouffe (see *hassock* UK)
hayseed	hick
haze *(verb)*	bully/upset
headed for	heading for +
heater (gas/electric)	gas fire/electric fire
heel (on the end of a loaf)	crust
heinie *(slang)*	buttocks
heist *(slang)*	robbery
hickey	lovebite
high roller	big spender +

For a guide to pronunciation symbols and other signs, see page vi.

US	UK
hike (at a slow pace)	ramble
hobo	tramp
hock	pawn +
hodgepodge	hotchpotch
hoedown	festive country dance
hogtied *(slang)*	restrained/thwarted
hokey	not credible/overly sentimental
holdover	relic +
holler	yell +
homebuilder	house builder
homely	plain/ugly (see *homely* UK)
homer *(colloq.)*	home run in baseball
homey *(slang)*	mate
hooch *(colloq.)*	cheap liquor
hood *(colloq.,* for *ruffian)*	hoodlum/tearaway
hood (on a car)	bonnet
hoof-and-mouth disease	foot-and-mouth disease
Hoosier	someone from Indiana
hooters *(vulgar slang)*	women's breasts (see *hooter* UK)
hope chest	bottomdrawer
horse blinders	horse blinkers
horse trailer	horsebox
horseback riding	horse riding
hot flash	hot flush
hot-dogger *(colloq.)*	stunt performer
housebroken	house-trained
hunker (down)	crouch +
hutch	dresser (see *dresser* US)

US	UK
hyphenated last name	double-barrelled surname
ID	identification
industrial park	trading estate
installment plan	hire purchase
Internal Revenue Service (IRS)	Inland Revenue
jackhammer	pneumatic drill +
jackrabbit	any of several species of large hares
jag	unrestrained expression of emotion
jam (verb)	play improvised music (usually as part of a group)
jammies (colloq.)	jim-jams
janitor	caretaker
java (slang)	coffee
Jell-O	jelly
jelly	jam +
jelly roll (the pastry)	Swiss roll
jemmy (verb)	jimmy +
jerk +	twerp/idiot +
jerky	dried strips of meat
joe (slang)	coffee
Joe Blow	Joe Bloggs
john* (slang)	loo
John Hancock (slang)	signature +
John boat	small, square-ended boat
josh (colloq.)	tease
jug*	large vessel usually with a cap
jump rope (noun)	skipping rope
jump rope (verb)	skip

For a guide to pronunciation symbols and other signs, see page vi.

US	UK
jumper	pinafore dress
jungle gym	climbing-frame
kerb store (regional)	corner shop
kerosene	paraffin
kibble	pelleted pet food
kibitz (*colloq.*, from Yiddish)	give unsolicited advice
kitty-corner/catty-corner	diagonally across
Klondike bar (brand name)	choc-ice
klutz (*colloq.*, from Yiddish)	clumsy person
knickers	knickerbockers
knock up *(offensive slang)*	make pregnant
kook *(colloq.)*	eccentric or crazy person
ladybug	ladybird
lanai (word of Hawaiian origin)	screened porch
landfill	amenity tip/dump +
landing gear	undercarriage
lap robe	rug* (light blanket)
last name +	surname
latex paint	emulsion paint
Laundromat	launderette
lavatory	basin/washroom
lawn bowling	bowls
layover	stopover
lazy Susan	dumb waiter*
lean-to	a shelter supported at one side by trees (see *lean-to* UK)
leash +	lead +
leery	wary + (see *leery* UK)

US	UK
legal holiday	bank holiday
liability insurance	third-party insurance
license plate	number-plate
life preserver	lifebuoy
life vest	life-jacket +
light bill *(colloq.)*	electricity bill
lightning bug	firefly +
lightning rod	lightning conductor
lima bean [**lī**·ma]	butter-bean
Limey (This slang term comes from the lime juice that was given to British sailors to prevent scurvy.)	a British person
line up	queue up
lineup (of suspects)	identity parade
Little Dipper (constellation)	Little Bear
liverwurst	liver sausage
loft	an open elevated area above the main level of a building (see *loft* UK); such a space used as a private flat (apartment)
lonesome (implies melancholy)	lonely +
longshoreman	docker +
lumber	timber
luminary	candle set in a bag in sand, used at night to guide the way (regional)
lush *(noun)*	drunkard
Mace (brand name)	CS gas
mail drop	letter-box

For a guide to pronunciation symbols and other signs, see page vi.

US	UK
main drag *(colloq.)*	main thoroughfare
maitre d'	head waiter
make out *(slang)**	snog/get off with someone
make over	do up
mall*	a large shopping center
man, dude (form of address)	mate
Marcite (brand name)	a compound used for surfacing swimming pools
marquee* (see *marquee* UK)	large, internally illuminated outdoor sign (such as seen outside cinemas)
mash (*verb*, Southern slang)	press
Masonite (brand name)	fibreboard
mat (around a picture)	mount
math	maths
maverick	unbranded calf/wild character
MC/master of ceremonies +	compère
mean	nasty (see *mean* UK)
measuring cup +	measuring jug
meat grinder	mincer
mechanical pencil	propelling pencil
medevac flight	mercy flight
median (on a road)	central reservation
Medicaid*	health-care program for indigents
Medicare*	federal health insurance program
merry-go-round (for children)	roundabout
midway	sideshow location at a fairground
milk can	milk churn
Milk-Bone (brand of dog biscuit)	Bonio

US	UK
misdemeanor	nonarrestable offense (similar)
mobile home	caravan
model home	show house
molasses	treacle
mom	mum
mom-and-pop *(adj.)*	family-owned
momentarily	in a moment (see *momentarily* UK)
monkey wrench (now obsolete)	adjustable spanner
motel	motor hotel, accessed by an exterior door
mother-in-law apartment	granny flat
mouth guard	gum-shield
movie theater	cinema +
MP	military police/redcap (see *redcap* US)
mudroom	vestibule used for removing soiled shoes/porch
mums *(colloq.)*	chrysanthemums
Murphy bed	foldaway bed
music box	musical box
muss up	mess up +
mutt *(slang)*	mongrel + (see *mutt* UK)
mutual fund	unit trust
nearsighted	short-sighted
neat *(colloq.)*	terrific
nerd	boring, studious person/square
nervy	cheeky/bold (see *nervy* UK)
New Year's	New Year's Eve

For a guide to pronunciation symbols and other signs, see page vi.

US	UK
newscaster	newsreader
newsstand	bookstall
night crawler (regional)	large worm
night school	evening classes
night stick	truncheon
nightgown	nightdress
nightstand/night table	bedside table
nipple (on a baby's bottle)	teat
nix *(verb)*	veto +
no-see-ums (regional)	biting midges
notarize	certify
nutcracker (at Christmas)	Russian sentinel doll
o.b.o. (or best offer)	o.n.o. (or near offer)
oarlock	rowlock [**rol**·lok]
oatmeal (cooked)	porridge
obstacle course (military)	assault course
one-way ticket	single ticket
open house (realtor's term)	house for sale that may be viewed
operator (alternative meaning)	devious/manipulative person
order of (in a restaurant)	portion of
ornery *(colloq.)*	difficult (person)
ottoman	footstool/pouffe
outhouse	outside toilet (see *outhouse* UK)
overseas +	abroad +
oxfords (shoes)	brogues
pacifier (for a baby)	dummy
pack rat	hoarder
package store	off-licence

US	UK
packinghouse	abattoir
paddle	spank +
paddle (table tennis)	bat
paddy wagon	Black Maria +
panhandler	beggar
panties	knickers
pantomime	show performed by a mime artist (see *pantomime* UK)
pants +	trousers +
pantyhose	tights
paper route	paper round
paraffin	paraffin wax +
paralegal	articled clerk (similar)
pardner *(slang)*	mate
pardon me	excuse me/pardon
parka +	anorak/windcheater
parking garage	multi-storey car park
parking lot	car park
part (in hair)	parting
pass-through	hatch
patsy	sucker +
pavement	road surface
Peace Corps	VSO (Voluntary Service Overseas)
peaked [**pee**·kid]	peaky
peg solitaire	solitaire
pen pal	pen-friend
penitentiary	prison +
period (punctuation)	full stop

For a guide to pronunciation symbols and other signs, see page vi.

US	UK
permit (for construction)	planning permission
pesky (slang)	annoying
phonograph	gramophone (see *phonograph* UK)
physical therapist	physiotherapist +
piazza (regional)	veranda/porch
picture ID	proof of identity and age with photograph
pigpen	pigsty +
pin (on lapel)	badge
pinkie	little finger
pinwheel (firework)	Catherine wheel
pissed *(vulgar)*	furious (see *pissed* UK)
pistol *(colloq.)*	lively person
pitcher	jug (see *jug* US)
Playbill (trademark)	theatre programme +
Play-Doh (brand name)	Plasticine (brand name)
player piano	Pianola (brand name)
plea bargain	an admission of guilt to a crime in exchange for a reduced sentence
Plexiglas (brand name)	Perspex (brand name)
plum pudding +	Christmas pudding
pocketbook*	financial resources/handbag
pole beans	stick beans
polliwog (regional)	tadpole +
pooch *(colloq.)*	lap-dog
pop/pa	dad +
Popsicle (brand name)	ice lolly
potholder	oven glove
potato chips	crisps

US	UK
pound/pound sign (the # symbol)	hash
pound cake	Madeira cake
preppy *(colloq.)*	a well-dressed preparatory school student (seen as typifying the upper and upper-middle classes)
principal	headmaster/headmistress +
prioritize *(colloq.)*	establish priorities
proctor	invigilator (see *proctor* UK)
produce [**prō**·doos]	greengroceries (fruit/vegetables)
professor	university lecturer or professor
(the) projects *(slang)*	council estate
property tax	council tax/rates
pry open	prise open
public housing project	council estate
public school	state school
public transportation	public transport
pudgy	podgy
pulp (in orange juice)	pith
pumped *(slang)*	excited
pumps (dress shoes for ladies)	court shoes
punkies (regional)	biting midges
purse	handbag
put out *(vulgar slang)*	make oneself sexually available to someone else; be sexually active
PX (Post Exchange)	NAAFI (Navy, Army, and Airforce Institutes)
Q-Tip (brand name)	cotton swab +
quiet down	quieten down

For a guide to pronunciation symbols and other signs, see page vi.

US	UK
quitting time	knocking-off time
Quonset hut (trademark)	Nissen hut (trademark)
quotation marks +	inverted commas
racetrack	racecourse +
rad *(hip slang)*	mad/brill
railroad	railway
railroad flat	a long, narrow flat
railroad *(verb, colloq.)*	to rush something in order to prevent objections or careful consideration
rain check	postponement ticket or invitation
raincoat +	mac/mackintosh
raise (in pay)	rise
raise (a child)	bring up +
ramada (regional Southwest)	shelter with wooden slats or thatched palms for a roof
rambunctious	rumbustious/rowdy/exuberant
range	cooker/stove
rap group	discussion group
rappel	abseil
rattle on *(slang)*	rabbit on/ramble on
ratty *(slang)*	tatty (see *ratty* UK)
razz *(slang)*	make fun of/rag
real-estate	property
realtor*/real-estate agent	estate agent
redcap	railway porter (see *redcap* UK)
redd up *(colloq., regional Midwest)*	tidy up
redneck* *(colloq.)*	oik/yobbo

US	UK
reform school +	Borstal
register (heating or cooling)	grille controlling air flow into a room
regular	normal/usual +
restroom	toilet/lavatory
resumé	c.v./curriculum vitae
roast + (cut of meat)	joint
Rolodex (brand name)	index card holder
romaine lettuce	cos lettuce
rookie *(colloq.)*	novice
roomer	lodger
ROTC (Reserve Officers' Training Corps)	CCF (Combined Cadet Force)
round-trip ticket	return ticket
route (delivery)	round
routing number	sort code
row house	terraced house
rubber *(colloq.)*	condom
rubber cement	cow gum
rubberneck *(verb, slang)*	gawk/turn and gaze (as at a traffic accident)
rubbing alcohol	isopropyl alcohol
ruckus	rumpus +
rug *(slang)*	hairpiece/toupee
rugrats *(derogatory slang)*	children
rumble *(colloq.)*	gang fight
run (in stockings)	ladder
runway (for modeling clothes)	catwalk

For a guide to pronunciation symbols and other signs, see page vi.

US	UK
rutabaga [**roo**·ta·bā·gə]	swede
S&H (shipping and handling)	P&P (postage and packing)
SPCA (Society for the Prevention of Cruelty to Animals)	RSPCA (Royal Society for the Prevention of Cruelty to Animals)
sailplane	glider +
salesperson	shop assistant
salesroom	saleroom
sandbox	sandpit
sanitary napkin	sanitary towel
Santa Claus +	Father Christmas
sappy	soppy
Saran Wrap (brand name)	cling film (plastic food wrap)
sassy (colloq.)	cheeky
scallion	spring onion
scalper	tout
scarf down	scoff down +
schedule (bus or train)	timetable +
schlep (regional slang)	slog/trudge/lug
schnoz (slang)	nose (especially a large one)
school (colloq.)	school, college, or university
schoolyard	school playground
scofflaw	a person who disregards the law
Scotch tape (brand name)	Sellotape (brand name)
scratch paper	scribbling block
secretary desk	bureau
seeds/pits (in fruit)	pips/stones
self-rising flour	self-raising flour
semester	half of an academic year

US	UK
server (in a restaurant)	waiter +
shade/window shade	blind
shades *(hip slang)*	sunglasses
shanty	shed/cabin
sharecropper	tenant farmer who gives a portion of each crop to the landowner in lieu of rent
sheers/sheer curtains	net curtains
Sheetrock (brand name)	plasterboard +
sherbet	sorbet [**sor**·bay] +
sheriff	chief of police outside city limits (see *sheriff* UK)
shill	someone who poses as a gambler or satisfied customer in order to encourage the participation or business of others
shin guard	shin-pad
shingle*	asphalt or wooden tile/small sign (see *shingle* UK)
shinny up	shin up +
shoeshine	the act of polishing shoes
Shoot!	Darn it!
shop *(colloq.)*	workshop/garage
short-order cook	cook in a basic restaurant
shower (bridal, baby)	women's gift-giving party prior to a big event
shrimp +	prawns +
shtick	comedian's or other entertainer's routine
shuck (oysters)	prise open

For a guide to pronunciation symbols and other signs, see page vi.

US	UK
shut-in	housebound person
shyster	unethical or unprofessional person (often a lawyer)
side (order)	side dish
sidewalk	pavement (see *pavement* US)
siding (on a building)	cladding
silent partner	sleeping partner
silverware	cutlery
skeeter (*slang,* regional South)	mozzie (*slang*)
ski mask	Balaclava
skillet	small frying pan
Skilsaw (brand name)	circular saw +
skinny-dipping	swimming nude
skivvies (*plural*)	underwear
skosh (*slang*) [skōsh]	a small amount
skycap	airport porter
slam-dunk *(noun)*	easy victory
slash (/) +	stroke/oblique
slate	set down for nomination/schedule an event (see *slate* UK)
slather	spread thickly
sled	toboggan
slew	a lot of
slicker	raincoat/mac
slim down	slim
slingshot	catapult +
slot machine	fruit machine (see *slot machine* UK)
smarts *(colloq.)*	intelligence
smoking gun	proof positive

US	UK
smudge pot	outdoor paraffin heater, used to protect plants from freezing weather
snake oil *(colloq.)*	quack remedy
snaps (fasteners)	press-studs
snap *(noun, colloq.)*	cinch +
sneakers	trainers
snippy	curt +/ratty (see *ratty* US)
snow peas +	mange-tout [**mahnzh**·too]
snowbird (informal)	a winter vacationer in the south
soccer ball	football
Social *(colloq.)*	Social Security Number
Social Security	old age pension/retirement pension (see *social security* UK)
sod +	turf +
soda (soft drink)	fizzy drink/pop +/soft drink +
soda cracker	water biscuit
soda fountain	snack bar in a general store
solicitor	canvasser
solitaire (card game)	patience (see *solitaire* UK)
some *(colloq.,* used at the end of a sentence)	a little
someplace	somewhere +
sow bug	woodlouse
soybeans	soya beans
Spackle (brand name)	Polyfilla (brand name)
spatula/pancake turner	fish slice/slice
specialty	speciality
Speedo (brand name)	brief swimming trunks for men

For a guide to pronunciation symbols and other signs, see page vi.

US	UK
spelunker (cave explorer)	potholer
spiffy	natty
spigot	outdoor tap/stopcock
spit up (of a baby)	vomit
split *(verb, slang)*	get moving/scarper
spook *(verb, colloq.)*	scare
spool of thread	reel of cotton
sport coat	sports jacket
square knot	reef-knot
squirrelly *(slang)*	eccentric/capricious
squirt gun	water pistol +
stall (in a restroom)	cubicle
stand-off	deadlock +
Stateside	in the US
STD (sexually transmitted disease)	VD/venereal disease + (see STD UK)
steamer trunk	trunk +
stick candy	rock/seaside rock
stiff *(verb, slang)*	fail to tip someone
stir-crazy *(slang)*	restless from confinement
stogy/stogie	a long, thin, inexpensive cigar
stoked *(slang)*	worked up
stool (alternative meaning)	toilet
stoop	porch +
store	shop or department store
storefront	retail outlet/shop window
storm window	secondary glazing (similar)
stove +	cooker

US	UK
straight pin	pin
straightaway (on a course)	straight
streetcar	tram
string beans	runner beans
stroke *(colloq.)*	compliment
stroller	pushchair/pram/perambulator
studly *(hip slang)*	handsome/macho
Styrofoam (brand name)	polystyrene/expanded polystyrene
subdivision	housing estate
substitute teacher	supply teacher
subway (train)	underground
sucker (candy on a stick)	lollipop +
surgery	operation + (see *surgery* UK)
suspenders	braces
swale	marshy depression
swan dive	swallow dive
swap meet (mostly used in the West)	sale of old cars and machinery at an outdoor venue/flea market
sweater set	twin set +
swimsuit +	bathing costume
swing shift	evening shift +
switchblade	flick-knife
table *(verb)*	put a bill or motion aside for discussion at a later time (see *table* UK)
tacky *(colloq.)*	tatty/tasteless +
taffy	small pieces of seaside rock
tag	label +

For a guide to pronunciation symbols and other signs, see page vi.

US	UK
tag (regional)	number plate/registration sticker
tag office (regional)	vehicle licence office +
tag sale	rummage sale
tailgate sale	boot sale
takeout (food)	take-away
talk show	chat show
tank (regional Texas)	pond
Tarheel	someone from North Carolina
tarp	tarpaulin +
tattletale *(noun, adj.)*	tell-tale
teakettle	kettle +
teamster	lorry driver
teardown (an old building)	knock-down
teeter-totter	seesaw +
telephone pole	telegraph pole
teller	cashier (in a bank or post office)
temblor	earthquake +
temple	synagogue +
thread	cotton +
thrift shop	charity shop
through (as in "Monday through Wednesday")	up to and including
throw (light blanket)	rug*
thumbtack	drawing-pin
thunderboomer *(colloq.)*	thunderstorm
tick off	annoy (see *tick off* UK)
tic-tac-toe	noughts and crosses
tidbit	titbit

US	UK
tightwad	stingy person
(to have a) tin ear	(to be) tone-deaf +
tire wrench	tyre lever
titled (used of a book)	entitled +
toilet bag	sponge bag
toll free	Freephone/Freefone
top off	top up
totaled (vehicle)	a write-off
toward +	towards +
track in (dirt)	tread in
trackless trolley	trolley bus +
trade	swap +
traffic circle	roundabout
trailer park	caravan site
training wheels	stabilizers (on a child's bike)
tram	parking lot conveyance (see *tram* UK)
tramp +	slut/down-and-out
transfer	ticket permitting a bus or train passenger to change to another vehicle to complete their journey
trapezium	trapezoid
trapezoid	trapezium
trash	rubbish
trash (*verb*)	destroy +
trash can	litter bin
trolley	tram/bus resembling a cable car
truck farmer	market gardener
trunk (on a car)	boot

For a guide to pronunciation symbols and other signs, see page vi.

US	UK
tube (electronic)	valve
tuckered out	knackered/fagged
tuck-point (to add mortar to brickwork)	point
tuition	college fees
turkey *(colloq.)*	an inept person/something that fails or does not meet expectations
turn signal (on a car)	indicator
turnkey (house or apartment/flat)	fully equipped
turnpike	toll-road +
turtleneck	polo-neck
tuxedo	dinner jacket
twister *(colloq.)*	tornado (see *twister* UK)
two-family	a property divided into two residences
Uncle Sam	the US government
undershirt	vest
upchuck *(slang)*	vomit
upcoming	forthcoming
upscale	upmarket
usher (in a church)	sidesman
utility bills	electricity/gas/water bills
VCR	video (player)
vacation	holiday
vacationer	holiday-maker
valance	pelmet (see *valance* UK)
vamoose *(slang)*	rush off
vanilla *(hip slang)*	ordinary

US	UK
vanity	dressing-table +
vaudeville	music hall
veg out [vej] *(hip slang)*	loll about
vest	waistcoat
vet*	war veteran/veterinary surgeon
Vienna sausage	small frankfurter
villa (regional East)	house within a condominium*
vine	creeper
visit with* *(colloq.)*	chat with/visit
Visquene (brand name)	heavy-duty plastic sheeting
volunteer work	voluntary work
vo-tech	technical institute
walk-up *(noun)*	above ground flat with no lift
wall-to-wall carpet	fitted carpet
want ad	newspaper classified advert
washcloth	flannel
wash the dishes	do the washing up
wash up	wash yourself (see *wash up* UK)
washroom (regional North)	public toilet
WASP	White Anglo-Saxon Protestant (often used disparagingly)
wastebasket	waste-paper basket
water cooler	cold-water dispenser
wax paper	greaseproof paper
wedding band	wedding ring +
Weed Whacker (brand name)	Strimmer (brand name)
welfare	social security (see *Social Security* US)
whipping cream	double cream

For a guide to pronunciation symbols and other signs, see page vi.

US	UK
whippoorwill	a variety of nightjar
whistle-stop	small town on a railway line
whitecaps (on water)	white horses
wiener [**wee**·ner]	frankfurter +
wind-up (of a toy)	clockwork
windbreaker	windcheater
Windex (brand name)	Windowlene (brand name)
windshield (on a car)	windscreen
Wite-Out (brand name)	Tippex (brand name)
witness stand	witness box
wood alcohol	methanol +
wuss [wûs]	wet or ineffectual person
Yankee	someone who lives north of the Mason-Dixon line, seen as the traditional boundary between the North and South of the US
yard*	garden (see *yard* UK)
yardman	gardener
yard work	gardening
yellow jacket	paper-wasp +
Zamboni (brand name)	ice-cleaning machine (on a rink)
zero +	nil/nought
zilch	nothing
zip *(slang)*	nothing
Zip Code	postcode
zipper	zip
zit	pimple
zucchini [zoo·**kee**·nee]	courgette [cor·**zhet**]

⊰ 17 ⊱

Explanations

Airing cupboard In the UK most houses have the hot-water storage tank in a small closet with shelves mounted above it. The shelves are made of wooden slats to allow the air to circulate. This keeps linens warm and dry. This is called the *airing cupboard.*

Appraise In the US a house is *appraised* by an *appraiser.* In the UK it is *valued* by a *valuer.* Conversely, job performance is usually *evaluated* in the US rather than *appraised* as it is in Britain.

Bikini The word *bikini* in the US can mean a man's brief swimsuit or a woman's two-piece swimsuit. In the UK it is only used in referring to a woman's two-piece swimsuit.

Billion This word can have two different meanings in the UK. One meaning is a million million: 1,000,000,000,000 or 10^{12}. The other meaning is the same as the meaning found in the US, a thousand million: 1,000,000,000 or 10^9. A thousand million has traditionally been called a *milliard* in Britain. To prevent confusion, in 1972 the British government began using the term *billion* to indicate 1,000,000,000 in its financial statistics. The older sense of *billion* seems to be going out of use in the UK, and the BBC (British Broadcasting Company) also now uses *billion* in the sense familiar to Americans.

Blowout A blowout has several meanings in the US. It can mean a tire suddenly losing air. It can also mean a big party. A blowout sale means a big sale with great price reductions.

Bollard A common word in British English, *bollard* can either mean a traffic diverter or a short upright metal post to secure a ship at a wharf. This word is only known in the US by nautical folk, for the latter meaning. It is unfamiliar to the average American.

Broil/Grill In the US *broiling* implies cooking something directly under the flame, while *grilling* implies cooking something over the flame. The term *grill* in the US may also mean frying something on a large, solid metal plate called a *grill*. In British English the word *grill* covers both the American words *broil* and *grill*. *Broasted* is an American word describing food that has been cooked in a high-pressure fryer made by the Broaster Company.

Bungalow In British English the word *bungalow* refers to any one-story house. A bungalow in the US indicates a small, modest one-story house, often made of wood and often prefabricated. Sears, Roebuck and Co. sold a mail-order bungalow kit known as a Craftsman bungalow between the years 1900 and 1930. These bungalows had built-in cupboards and bookcases.

Café The word *café* in American English can mean "nightclub" as well as "coffee shop."

Call If an American says "They're calling for rain," he means the forecast indicates that rain is likely. If a thermostat is set high enough for the heat to come on, the thermostat is said to be *calling for heat*.

Can In the UK one *bottles* fruit, often in a Kilner jar. In the US one *cans* fruit, often in a Mason jar.

Cheers This is sometimes used as a toast before taking a drink in the US. In the UK, however, *cheers* is often used as a friendly, informal way of saying thanks. The American *Thanks, buddy* might be translated as *Cheers, mate*. Britons also frequently end informal e-mails with *Cheers* before their signature or initial.

Chemist In the UK *chemist* can refer to a laboratory chemist, a pharmacist, or the pharmacy itself.

Cider In the UK cider is an alcoholic beverage. In the US cider is usually unfermented apple juice but *hard cider* is alcoholic.

Condominium/Condo (From the Latin words *com-* "with" and *dominium* "domain.") In the US, this common word indicates a complex of individually owned houses or apartments whose owners belong to a legal association for the proper and continued maintenance of all commonly owned property on which their residences are located. The term refers either to the entire complex or to a single unit in the complex. Owners often time-share or lease their condos to others.

Cool Americans use *cool* in a variety of ways. It can mean "modern, liberal, up-to-date" (*She's cool, That's cool*) or "acceptable, not a threat, in-the-know" (*He's cool*), or it can be an exclamation of approval, appreciation, or delight (*Cool!*).

Cornfield A cornfield in the US is a field of maize. A cornfield in the UK, however, is a field of wheat or oats. Maize is not grown on a large scale in the UK.

Crack If an American asks you to *crack* a window, he wants you to open it slightly.

Crazy The British term *crazy paving* is as perplexing to most Americans as the term *crazy quilt* is to most Britons. In both cases the term *crazy* means *patchwork.*

Cross ventilation In the US, a room is said to have good *cross ventilation* if it has windows at opposite ends, permitting a good movement of air through the room.

Disassemble In the US *disassemble* and *dismantle* are often used interchangeably regarding something tangible, such as a tent. However, one *dismantles* a regime or a social service. In the UK only the verb *dismantle,* never *disassemble,* is used.

Drapes *Drapes* and *draperies* are both used for "curtains" in the US. *Draperies* is considered the preferred word by some people, but *drapes* is still the more common word. The term *window treatments* covers all the material at a window. Curtains in the US usually do not draw.

Drugstore/Pharmacy While these terms are often used interchangeably in the US, there is a distinction to be made. A *pharmacy* is a section in a large department store, while a *drugstore* is a separate or privately owned shop.

Dumbwaiter/Dumb waiter In both countries, a *dumbwaiter* (*dumb waiter* in the UK) is a device for transporting food between floors. However, in Britain, *dumb waiter* can also mean a revolving food holder at a dining table. This object is known as a *lazy Susan* in the US.

Duplex The word *duplex* (also known as a *two-family*) refers to two semi-detached single houses on one lot. The houses are often separated in the middle by two garages. Duplexes are often rental properties. In some areas a duplex may be two rental properties, one above the other.

Guy If used in the plural this word can refer to men *and* women in the US.

Hire/Rent The terms *hire* and *rent* are often used interchangeably in Britain. However, in the US *hire* refers to people, while *rent* usually refers to things, such as a videotape or car. *Lease* implies a long-term legal obligation in the renting of items. The term *let* has pretty much fallen from popular use in the US. Normally the term *rent out* is used instead of the term *let*, although *rent* alone is often used. The distinctions in meaning are easily understood in context.

Holiday A *holiday* or *legal holiday* in the US is usually what the British call a *bank holiday*. The expression *the holidays* in the US generally refers to the period between Thanksgiving, which occurs at the end of November, and New Year's Day. *Vacation* is the usual equivalent of the British word *holiday*.

Hospital In Britain, if one is admitted, one goes *to hospital.* If one is visiting a patient, one goes *to the hospital.* In the US, there is no distinction. It is always *the* hospital. Similarly, Americans say "The child is in the hospital," rather than "The child is in hospital," when the child is receiving treatment there.

Icing and Frosting These words are often used interchangeably in the US, although more accurately *icing* refers to a smooth topping and *frosting* to a whipped or creamy topping. *Frosting* is not used in Britain.

John The word *john,* in the US, has several meanings. The *john* means the toilet (originally a term used for an outdoor toilet for men, the women's being the *Jane*). A *john* also means a hooker's (prostitute's) client (*punter* in British English). A *dear John letter* is a letter requesting a divorce or the end of a relationship.

Jug A *jug* in British English would be known as a *pitcher* in American English. A jug in the US is a large vessel with a handle and a narrow neck, usually with a stopper.

Knock up The phrase *knock up* can be used in a variety of ways in British English. One can *knock up* a person, meaning wake them up. One can *knock up* at tennis (warm up). One can *knock up* a meal in a hurry, and one can even *knock oneself up* (knock oneself out). The only meaning of *knock up* in American English is a vulgar slang expression meaning *to make a woman pregnant.*

Luminary In both countries, the word *luminary* can mean a leader in a scientific field or artistic profession. In the US, especially in the South, this word is also used to mean a candle set inside a paper bag for illuminating a path at night. These candles are also called *luminarias,* which is a Spanish word.

Mail In general, the word *mail* may be substituted in the US for the British term *post.* However, there are some exceptions, such as *postmark, post office,* and *the postal service.*

Mains Water and electricity are shut off at the *main* in the US, but at the *mains* in Britain. The term *mains pressure* (for water) might just be called the *water pressure* or simply the *pressure* in the US, as in "The water pressure on the upper floors was low." The relative terminology reflects differences between the US and the UK in the hot and cold water systems usually found in houses. The expression *run off the mains* (for electricity) has no good equivalent in the US.

Mall, Plaza In the US a *plaza* [**plah**·za] is a shopping center with a collection of individual shops and stores sharing parking facilities. A *mall* [mawl] is a collection of individual shops and stores constructed under one roof with a common indoor, air-conditioned, or heated promenade. It is usually much larger than a plaza, and contains a mixture of large department stores and smaller shops and restaurants.

Marquee The word *marquee* probably originated in a false attempt at making a singular word from *marquise* around 1680. *Marquee* was originally used for a shelter for a marquis or marquise. The word came to mean a large outdoor tent in British English, and an awning projecting over an entrance in American English. Younger Americans tend to use the word mostly to describe an illuminated sign either over a theatre or by the road.

Medicare/Medicaid *Medicare* is a US government program of medical insurance for people age 65 or older and some people under age 65 who are sick or disabled. *Medicaid* is a federal and state program for people with low incomes.

Pocketbook This word is mostly used by older Americans to mean a handbag, also called a purse in the US. To younger Americans the term is usually applied to financial resources, as in "That white sports car is too much for my pocketbook."

Porch A porch in England is a small sheltered area outside a building. It is similar to a *mudroom* in the US. An American porch can be a much larger, often elevated area at the front or back of the house where one can sit. This would be called a *verandah* in Britain.

Precinct The word *precinct* is used in very specific but different ways. A *pedestrian precinct* in British English is a shopping district in a town or city where vehicles are not permitted. In the US *precinct* refers to a district within the jurisdiction of a fire or police department.

Realtor The word *Realtor* is trademarked, although it often appears lowercase. It refers to a real estate agent who is a member of the National Association of Realtors. It is commonly used by Americans to refer to any real estate agent.

Redneck This slang term, which can be quite offensive, refers to an intractable, crude person with set ideas and opinions. It may also connote a lack of education or intelligence, but not necessarily. The word itself was originally a deprecatory term for white laborers in the South who had sunburned necks from bending over in the fields.

Rug In the UK the word *rug* can be used to describe a light blanket used to cover oneself, or to sit on at a picnic. This is known in the US as a *throw*. A large carpet may be referred to as a *rug* in the US. In American English, a *rug* is also a slang term for a hairpiece.

Sale In the US, the word *sale* is used in many ways:

blowout sale	clearance sale
closeout sale	closing-down sale
garage sale	sale of used household items held outdoors or in a garage
tag sale	same as the British jumble sale
trunk sale	sale of last season's merchandise in a clothing store
yard sale	same as a garage sale

Shingle A *shingle* in the US is either an asphalt or wooden tile or a small sign outside a business—quite different from the British meaning of beach pebbles.

Tap A tap in the house is known as a *faucet* in the US. An outdoor tap or a stopcock is called a *spigot*. However, water from the faucet is called *tap water*.

Teeth The Brits *clean* their teeth, whereas the Americans *brush* their teeth. *Teeth cleaning* in the US is done at the dentist's office.

Toboggan A *toboggan* in the US is a specific kind of sled without runners and with a front that curves up. *Sled* is the US term for the British word *toboggan*.

Vet The word *vet* in the US can either mean a veterinarian or a war veteran. In Britain it is an abbreviation for *veterinary surgeon*.

Visit with In the US, this can either mean "visit" in the British sense (to go and socialize with), or it can be used in place of to *chat with*. It is a rather informal expression.

Warden In British English, the term *warden* refers to the governor of a hospital, college, or YMCA. A prison governor is called a *warden* in American English.

Whistle stop A *whistle stop* is a small town along a railway line in the US. It can also mean a short appearance by a performing group or a politician in such a town.

Yard The word *yard* in the US refers to the area around a house and roughly equates to the British word *garden*. The word *garden* in the US is used in reference to a cultivated area such as a rose garden or a vegetable garden, in contrast to other areas around the house where only grass, landscaping bushes, and trees grow. A *yard* in British English is a paved area.

⇥ 18 ⇤

Other Varieties of English

British English is spoken in many countries as a second language, although South Americans usually learn American English. Here are some terms that are only found in Canada, Australia, New Zealand, and South Africa.

CANADA

English and French are the two official languages of Canada. The English spoken in Canada strongly resembles American English, although the spelling conforms in large part to British English. Words such as *car park, cutlery, holiday* (a *vacation* in the US), *jelly, porridge, serviette, tick* (a *check mark* in the US), *till,* and *top up* are a reminder of Canada's links to Britain. Canadians often use the British pronunciations when it comes to words such as *process* and *project.*

Canadian Terms

CANADIAN TERM	MEANING
ABM (Automatic Bank Machine is occasionally seen as well as ATM)	ATM/cash machine
blue box	recycling bin
boxliner (in the bed of a pick-up)	bedliner
broadloom	wall-to-wall carpet
canopy (over the bed of a pick-up)	topper
chesterfield	sofa or couch (used mostly by older Canadians)
chip wagon (regional)	van at the side of the road from which French fries are sold
CPP (Canadian Pension Plan)	Social Security (US)/OAP (UK)
fire hall	fire station
Garburator (brand name)	kitchen waste disposer
had the biscuit (as in "He's had the biscuit.")	had it (as in "He's had it. He's finished.")
hydro	electricity (often generated from hydroelectric plants)
Inuit/N. Aboriginal people/ First Nations	Eskimo (The term *Inuit* is preferred to *Eskimo* by many groups of indigenous Arctic peoples.)
Joe Lunchpail	blue-collar worker
landed immigrant	a foreigner who is a legal resident of Canada, but is not a Canadian citizen
laneway	alleyway

CANADIAN TERM	MEANING
Mountie	a member of the RCMP (similar to a federal law enforcement officer in the US)
on pogey *(slang)*	unemployed
parkade	multilevel parking structure
provincial	pertaining to a Canadian province or to the provinces (This is the main meaning in Canada, rather than "countrified" or "parochial.")
RCMP	Royal Canadian Mounted Police
riding	constituency/electoral district
RRSP	Registered Retirement Savings Plan (similar to an IRA in the US)
SIN	Social Insurance Number (similar to a Social Security Number in US)
washroom	restroom/lavatory

AUSTRALIA

Australian English closely resembles British English in the written form, although some of the slang terms that are commonplace in everyday speech in Australia can sound quite strange to a Briton. Some accents resemble British speech, whereas broader accents are typified by the *oi* sound for the long *i* as in *fine* [foin]. Where other varieties of English have the long *a* vowel [ā], broader Australian accents may have a sound like long *i* [ī]. The broad Australian pronunciation of word *hate* may thus sound like the word *height* to Americans and Britons. From a Briton's point of view, regional accents in Australia are not very great despite the large size of the country—although regional variation does exist, such as in the names for the different sizes of beer glasses. Australians love their beer, which is generally served in jugs (pitchers in the US), and beer glasses have interesting names. A *schooner* is usually 15 ounces, a *butcher* is 7 ounces, and a *pony* is 5 ounces.

Australian Terms

AUSTRALIAN TERM	MEANING
Aussie [ozzy]	an Australian *(noun)*/Australian *(adj.)*
bag	criticize
barrack for *(verb)*	cheer for (a team)
Beauty!	Terrific!
Besser Block (brand name)	cinderblock
big smoke, the	a large city
bludger	someone who lives off others
blue	mistake/fight
bluey	summons (to a court)
bonzer	terrific
bower-bird	pack rat/hoarder
brumby	wild horse
bullbar (on a car)	grille guard (US)
bung it on	put on airs
bunyip	mythical people-eating monster
bushwacker	unrefined country person
chaulkie	schoolteacher
chook [chûk]	chicken
cobber (old-fashioned)	pal
cocky	farmer
cossie [coz·zy]	bathing suit
crook	sick
dag	dull person

AUSTRALIAN TERM	MEANING
dobber	informant
docket	sales slip
domain	park
dunny	outhouse/outside toilet
ear-bash *(verb)*	harangue
Esky (brand name)	cooler/ice chest
fair dinkum *(adj.)*	genuine
Fair dinkum!	You don't say!
freezing works	slaughterhouse
first up	firstly
G'day!	Hi!
Good as gold!	Doing fine!
hard yakka	hard work
home and hosed	safely completed
home unit	condominium
Hooray! (regional)	Goodbye!
hotel *(colloq.)*	bar
jackaroo/jilaroo (female)	novice on a sheep or cattle station
larrikin	hooligan
lash	bash/try
metal road	dirt road
ocker/okker	unrefined Australian man
over the fence	unreasonable
paddock	field
pawpaw	papaya +
poker machines/pokies	slot machines (US)/fruit machines (UK)
pom/pommie	someone from Britain
port (regional Queensland)	suitcase

AUSTRALIAN TERM	MEANING
postie *(colloq.)*	postman
prime mover	truck cab and engine (on a cab and trailer vehicle)
retrenched	laid off from work
sand-shoes	tennis shoes
screw *(colloq.)*	prison guard
sealed road	paved road
She's right!/She'll be right!	It's all right!
sheila *(slang)*	girl
smoko	coffee break
squiz *(noun)*	peek
station	ranch/large farm
stickybeak	nosy person
strides	trousers
Strine (from *'Stralian*)	uncultivated Australian speech
stubbie	beer bottle (small)
this arvo	this afternoon
tinnie	beer can
tip-truck	tipper truck
truckie	trucker
tucker	food
ute/utility truck	pick-up
verandah (additional meaning)	solid awning over the front of retail outlets
Wait on!	Hang on (a minute)!
weekender	weekend cottage
wharfie	stevedore/docker
(the) wog	prevailing cold virus

AUSTRALIAN TERM	MEANING
Woop Woop	the middle of nowhere
yabbies	tiny crayfish

For a guide to pronunciation symbols and other signs, see page vi.

NEW ZEALAND

New Zealand English is also very similar to British English in the written form. New Zealanders think they speak in a more refined manner than Australians, but the average foreigner would be hard-pressed to tell the difference. Rising inflection is also common there. A short *i* (as in *lift*) often has a distinctive schwa-like sound. The short *e* often sounds like a long *e*, hence *set* and *seat* can sound similar to someone not from New Zealand.

New Zealand Terms

NEW ZEALAND TERM	MEANING
batch	weekend cottage
blue	mistake
(the) Bot	prevailing cold virus
butchery	butcher's shop
cattle-stop	cattle-grid (UK)/cattle guard (US)
Chilly Bin (brand name)	cooler/ice chest
chook [chûk]	chicken
dairy	convenience store
dobber	informant
docket	sales slip
domain	park
emergency (in a team sport)	substitute/alternate
Fred Dagg	unrefined New Zealander

For a guide to pronunciation symbols and other signs, see page vi.

NEW ZEALAND TERM	MEANING
haka	Maori ceremonial dance
Jandals (brand name)	flip-flops
kiwi [**kee**·wee]	flightless New Zealand bird/ a person from New Zealand
paddock	field
pakeha [**pah**·kay·hah]	white (non-Maori) person (The Maori are the indigenous people of New Zealand.)
pavlova [păv·**loh**·va]	a meringue cake filled with fruit, cream, and ice cream
section	plot of land
sheila	girl
smoko	coffee break
strides	trousers

SOUTH AFRICA

Written South African English is also similar to British English. Spoken South African English has a vague resemblance to New Zealand English with the short *e* sounding almost like a long *e*. Here are a few interesting words that are unique to this country.

South African Terms

SOUTH AFRICAN TERM	MEANING
bakkie [**buk**·ky]	pick-up truck
bioscope (old-fashioned)	cinema
boetie	brother/buddy
bottle store	liquor store
braai [bry] *(noun, verb)*	barbecue

For a guide to pronunciation symbols and other signs, see page vi.

SOUTH AFRICAN TERM	MEANING
Catch me a brew!	Give me a beer!
china (see Cockney Rhyming Slang, page 238).	friend/acquaintance
donder [donn·er]	wallop
donga [**don**·ga]	hole in the ground
drift	ford/causeway
It's tickets!	It's curtains!
just now	in a short while
larney	posh
lekker	tasty/good
naartjie [**nah**·chee]	tangerine
okie/outjie [**o**·kie]	buddy
ous [ohz] *(plural)*	folks
packet	bag
robot	traffic light
rondavel [ron·**dah**·vəl]	a traditional African dwelling consisting of a circular hut with a thatched roof (This style is now used as accommodation at game reserves and many holiday resorts.)
Shame!	Too bad!/How precious!/How darling!
spanspeck/sponspek	cantaloupe
takkies	canvas shoes
veld [felt]	open grassland
veldskoen [**felt**·skoon]	soft leather shoe that comes up over the ankle

⊰ 19 ⊱

Cockney Rhyming Slang

Since the sixteenth century Cockney rhyming slang has been heard in the East End of London. Its origins are somewhat obscure, but it allowed workers to hold a private conversation within their ranks without the bosses knowing what they were talking about. The person speaking uses a rhyming word or expression like a code to replace the word he or she really means to say. For example, *whistle and flute* is used to stand for *suit*. When it is shortened to *whistle,* it becomes even more obscure, because the rhyming word is not there from which to guess the meaning. In the beginning Cockney rhyming slang was mainly used by seamen and itinerant laborers, but it is now used by many blue-collar Londoners. It not only includes an extensive number of expressions but is constantly changing like many other aspects of language. Below is a representative sample.

Cockney Rhyming Slang

RHYMING SLANG EXPRESSION	MEANING
apples and pears	stairs
April showers	flowers
Auntie Ella	umbrella
bacon and eggs	legs

RHYMING SLANG EXPRESSION	MEANING
Baden Powell	towel
Barnet (Barnet fair)	hair
bird (bird lime)	time (in prison)
boat (boat race)	face
bread (bread and honey)	money
bread and butter	gutter
bucket and pail	jail
bull and cow	row (an argument)
butcher's-hook	look
canoes	shoes
china (china plate)	mate
daft and barmy	army
daisy roots	boots
dicky bird	word
dig in the grave	shave
dog and bone	phone
donkey's ears	years
dustbin lids	kids
fine and dandy	brandy
frog and toad	road
ginger beer	queer (odd)
gold watch	scotch
half inch	pinch (to steal)
Hampstead Heath	teeth
hit and miss	kiss
Holy Ghost	toast
horse and carriage	marriage
jam jar	car

RHYMING SLANG EXPRESSION	MEANING
loaf (loaf of bread)	head
marbles (marbles and conkers)	bonkers (See *conkers* in UK–US lexicon.)
Mother Hubbard	cupboard
near and far	bar
north and south	mouth
old bag	hag
on the floor	poor
Peckham Rye	tie
pen (pen and ink)	stink
Persian rugs	drugs
pillar and post	ghost
pitch and toss	boss
plates of meat	feet
pork pies	lies
rabbit (rabbit and pork)	talk (*pork* rhymes with *talk* in UK)
read and write	fight
rub-a-dub-dub	pub
sausage and mash	cash
sky rocket	pocket
tea leaf	thief
ten-speed gears	ears
titfer (tit for tat)	hat
Toby jug	mug (fool)
tod (Tod Sloane)	alone (on one's tod)
toe rag	slag (prostitute)/fag (cigarette)
two and eight	in a state

Afterword

Many people who speak British English feel that American English is taking over as a form of global communication, and they may be right. The Internet is dominated by American websites that naturally promote American English. The Commonwealth and former Commonwealth countries comprise a huge number of speakers of different varieties of English, and in many ways people living in these countries feel somewhat threatened by American English. Many consider American English to be rather sloppy, and they are concerned that American spelling may dominate and somehow contaminate their language.

Americans often accept these attitudes uncritically and consider British English to be the proper or real English. But the differences between American English and the other varieties do not result from sloppiness. Since the United States gained independence from Britain much earlier than most other former colonies, American English has had longer to develop separately from British English than other varieties. In more recent times, the immigration and trade ties among Britain, India, New Zealand, Australia and South Africa have been stronger than those between Britain and America, even though America is geographically closer to the British Isles. Noah Webster also helped shape the spelling differences between British and American English through his *American Dictionary of the English Language,* which became the main reference source for many US school teachers and newspaper editors back in the 1800s. Spelling reform has taken place in Britain too, most noticeably with the preference for *–ise* suffix in words such as *apologize* and *realize.*

Although new words from American English (many of them slang) creep into British English subtly but surely each year, I cannot foresee a day anytime soon when an Englishman will use the term *check mark* instead of a *tick* on his to-do list or call a *full stop* a *period* when dictating notes. In some ways British English is even gaining ground. In India, for example, many recently coined British terms have been adopted, like *LGV* as the word for a large truck. I have a hunch that British English will be around for many years to come.

Even though the relationship between American English and other varieties of English in the world is often depicted as a fight to the finish between us and them (or between us and the US!), in all fairness I cannot say that one version of English is superior to the other. From America to South Africa to Australia, English-speaking people around the globe can learn to understand each other quite well with a little effort and help from books like this one. In this sense, the United Kingdom and its former colonies, including the United States, remain united by a common language.

Index

Readers who wish to find a specific word or phrase in British or American English should first consult the three large lexicons in Chapters 12, 15 and 16. If the expression cannot be found in these lexicons, readers can use this index to find words and phrases discussed elsewhere in the book.